George D. Cearley Jr.
4449 Goodfellow Dr
Dallas Texas, 75229

or PO Box 12312
Dallas, Texas 75225

phone: 214-352-2212

D1293547

The Pocket Encyclopedia of World Aircraft in Color

AIRLINERS
SINCE 1946

The Pocket Encyclopedia
of World Aircraft in Color

AIRLINERS

SINCE 1946

by
KENNETH MUNSON

Illustrated by
JOHN W. WOOD

Michael Baber
Frank Friend
Brian Hiley
William Hobson
Alan Holliday
Jack Pelling
Allen Randall

THE MACMILLAN COMPANY

THE MACMILLAN COMPANY
866 Third Avenue, New York, N.Y. 10022

Color section printed in Holland by Ysel Press Ltd.
Text printed and books bound in Great Britain by
Richard Clay (The Chaucer Press) Ltd., Bungay, Suffolk

PREFACE

TO THE FIRST REVISED EDITION

In the four and a half years which have elapsed since the original edition of this volume appeared, the commercial air transport scene has reflected a number of major changes. Among these are the virtual extinction of the piston-engined airliner from the fleets of the major operators; the entry into service of the Boeing 747, the first of the new generation of 'jumbo' jets; the marked rise in the fortunes of 'third-level' or commuter airline operators; and, perhaps most important of all, the sociological challenge posed by the supersonic passenger transport, opposition to which caused the cancellation of the United States' SST programme early in 1971. Meanwhile, the sales of subsonic jet airliners continue to rise, albeit less quickly, and during the next few years the new generation of wide-bodied 'airbus' transports will begin to enter service.

In this first revised edition, nine new aircraft appear for the first time, nearly a dozen other colour plates have been revised or updated, and the text also has been completely updated throughout.

No publication of this kind can ever be compiled without assistance and encouragement from a wide variety of sources, and I owe no small debt of gratitude to the many aircraft manufacturers, airline and business operators who supplied valuable reference material. Among a host of individual helpers, particular mention must be given to Messrs Norman Rivett and Brian Service, whose extensive collections of colour slides were an invaluable aid. My thanks for their assistance must also go to Messrs James Halley, Michael Hooks and John Wickenden of Air-Britain, to Maurice Allward, Mário Roberto Vaz Carneiro, Olle Hagblom of SAS, Stephen Peltz, Profile Publications Ltd and John W. R. Taylor.

October 1971

INTRODUCTION

THE AIR transport scene after the end of World War 2 was a motley one indeed. Most of the available aircraft plant in Europe had been turning out warplanes at the direction of the Axis dictators; Britain and Russia, too, had concentrated their efforts on mass production of the more militant types. Thus, only the United States had been able to maintain a continuity of transport aircraft production since the pre-war era. With her massive resources she had been able to sustain, for four years, the output of enough aircraft to meet virtually the entire transportation needs of all the major Allied powers: a fact which gave her a marked advantage over the other aircraft-producing nations at the war's end. With the tremendous run-down of military forces that immediately followed, many thousands of war-surplus transports became readily available for sale to airline operators both inside and outside the United States. These aeroplanes had already proved their capabilities under operational conditions far more arduous than any they would meet in peacetime, and so could be put straight into service once their interiors had been 'civilianised'. Furthermore, although many of them had not been developed with operating economics uppermost in mind, their availability provided a valuable breathing space while types with better commercial attributes were designed and tested.

Not all of the aircraft used by airlines during the mid-1940s started their lives as pure transports, however. The mainstay of the French internal and international networks, for instance, was for several years the veteran Junkers Ju 52/3m, designed nearly a decade and a half earlier as a Luftwaffe bomber and only diverted to transport duties after its shortcomings as a bomber had been revealed during the Spanish civil war. Bombers of more recent design, too, were obvious targets for stop-gap conversion to passenger- and freight-carrying duties, because of their size and their ability to fly long distances. The US Flying Fortress and Liberator, and Britain's Halifax and Lancaster, all underwent conversion in this way. Their comparatively modest payloads made them costly to operate, and from an economic viewpoint it was as well that they were only short-term equipment for the larger airlines; but their contribution to the Berlin airlift a year or two later was beyond price. One bomber development that deserves separate mention is the Boeing Stratocruiser, for this descendant of the B-29 Superfortress can justly be regarded as a true airliner in its own right, and its interior appointments for the comfort and safety of its passengers in flight set new standards that were not matched by any other type for several years.

Meanwhile, the latter half of the 1940s saw the gradual emergence of new airliner designs, or developments of older ones, that had been growing on the drawing boards since the middle years of the war. In Britain these were geared chiefly to the recommendations of the Brabazon Committee, and the aeroplanes that eventually resulted from the requirements laid down by this committee met with widely differing degrees of success. The Dove and Viscount, for example, subsequently proved to be first-class money-spinners; rather less fortune attended the Ambassador and the Marathon, while the giant Brabazon suffered the penalty of being ahead of its time and the ignominy of being reduced to scrap after only a few hundred hours in the air.

For many years the four-engined airliner market was largely taken care of by the progressively developed Douglas DC-4/6/7 series and the Lockheed Constellation/Super Constellation range, both originated before and developed during the war. In the realm of the short/medium-range twin-engined airliner, however, despite the numerical preponderance of war-surplus C-46's and C-47's, several new designs began to emerge during the late 1940s and early 1950s. The principal British contender in this field was the Vickers Viking, a tubby but efficient and hardworking design that was a familiar sight on the European networks until the middle 1950s. The more elegant Ambassador also sustained the popularity which attended its introduction by BEA in 1952, and its built-in passenger appeal was surpassed only by the Viscount among post-war British propeller-driven airliners. In retrospect it may be considered a great pity that only about a score of them were built. The fact that fifteen were still in active airline service at the end of 1966 speaks highly for the aeroplane's safety record, as well as for its popularity; and the two factors are not without

8

connection. A similar observation might be made in regard to the Swedish Scandia, another medium twin also built only in modest numbers yet with a service record extending into the late 1960s.

In the Soviet Union, the veteran designer Sergei Ilyushin made his contribution to the medium twin scene, first with the interim Il-12 design and later with the Il-14. The latter, in terms of length and breadth of service, of numbers built and of duties performed, well deserves to be called 'the Russian DC-3', and has been the staple equipment of many Communist bloc airlines, not to mention military squadrons, for much of the post-war period.

The US aviation industry produced two major types in this category, namely the Martin 2-0-2 and the Convair 240. The former, and its derivative the Martin 4-0-4, were built in comparatively modest numbers by US standards, and their employment was confined largely to the Americas. The Convair 240, on the other hand, was ordered extensively by both military and civil customers and its development continued into the second half of the 1960s, following the alliance of its well-proven airframe with the latest turboprop engines.

It was of course the Vickers Viscount which really brought home to the airlines the virtues of turboprop powerplants, and subsequently it became not only the first but – until overtaken in more recent times by the twin-Dart-powered Friendship – by far the most successful airliner since the war to be powered in this fashion. The Americans, curiously, did not pursue the application of the turboprop to passenger aircraft to the degree that might have been expected of a world leader in air transport design. While the Viscount was fast establishing new standards of speed, comfort and efficiency, the US aero-engine industry was still wringing the last ounce of energy out of the piston engine in the form of the Wright Turbo Compound that powered its DC-7s and Super Constellations. The only American airliner designed from the outset for propeller-turbine engines was the Electra, which entered service some years later than the Viscount and in less than half the numbers.

Apart from Britain, where the Viscount and Hawker Siddeley 748, and the larger Britannia and Vanguard, have fully demonstrated the efficacy of the turboprop engine, the only other nation really to pursue it in relation to large passenger-carrying aircraft has been the USSR. So much so, in fact, that the Soviet Union has the most powerful propeller-turbine engines in the world: those installed in the giant Tu-114 each develop nearly 15,000 shp, while those of the An-22 military freighter are more powerful still. Russian designers, and Oleg Antonov in particular, chose turbo-prop powerplants for a considerable range of new civil aircraft which began to appear in the mid-1950s. Most of these are used within the Soviet Union, where the turboprop's economy with heavy loads over long distances, and its less demanding runway requirements than the pure jet, are important factors in its favour.

France, despite its considerable success in other categories of aviation, has made comparatively little impact on the turboprop transport scene, the twin-Bastan N 262/Frégate having mustered only about fifty sales in seven years. Greater success has attended the Japanese designed and built YS-11, which relies on that most proven of all propeller-turbines, the Rolls-Royce Dart.

As with the turboprop, so with the turbojet, and the first jet airliner on the scene was also of British design. The wartime Bra-bazon Committee was inclined to be somewhat reticent about the potentialities of the jet engine in relation to mass passenger transport; or perhaps it felt that the development costs of a large inter-continental jet airliner would be too prohibitive for a nation still recovering from the unprecedented expense of the war. At any rate, its Type IV recommendations related only to a medium-range jet transport with modest payload capabilities, and it was left to de Havilland to prove that a larger machine could compete with propeller-driven transports on the Empire routes. In 1952 the Comet proudly entered service with BOAC; the tragic accidents and subsequent grounding of all Comets in 1954 are now a matter of history, and it was another four and a half years before the much-improved Comet 4 took the place of its forebear. True, it still beat the Boeing 707 into service across the North Atlantic, and the intervening years were far from being entirely wasted; but they still represented much lost time, one of the commodities least dispensable to any aviation industry.

Meanwhile, the distinction of being the second jetliner into service had gone, not to America, as might have been expected, but to the Soviet Union, whose twin-jet Tu-104 had taken the western nations by surprise early in 1956 and entered service inside Russia a year later. Some western observers, seeming almost to take the Tu-104's existence as a personal affront, dwelt heavily on the fact that it was 'only a converted bomber', and ridiculed the Victorian-style décor of the passenger accommodation; but the Tu-104 was no prestige lash-up, as its subsequent years of airline service have demonstrated beyond question.

At last, in October 1958, the first American jetliner, the now ubiquitous Boeing 707, entered service across the North Atlantic. Pan American was the pioneer airline, but a comparable fleet of Boeings had simultaneously been ordered by PanAm's great rival, Trans World Airlines, and this was to spark off the greatest and most expensive one-upmanship race in the history of aviation. Rightly or wrongly – we shall never know – airline after airline decided that it would have to have jets itself or go out of business, and the Boeing order book grew almost daily. For almost a year the Seattle manufacturer had things virtually all its own way, for its greatest rival, Douglas, was not to have the competing DC-8 in service until September 1959. Since then both American types have grown into 'families' of jet airliners with a variant for almost every conceivable route requirement.

One by-product of the great scramble for jet equipment was that the secondhand airliner market began to receive a glut of redundant but by no means retirement-worthy piston-engined aircraft. As a result, quite a few less affluent (or less hot-headed) airlines found themselves in a buyers' market where they could discard piston-engined aircraft that had worn out and replace them at an unexpectedly low cost with similar or better machines that still had plenty of service left in them. One such airline, Icelandair, was even able to make advertising capital of the fact that it was the only *non*-jet airline flying the North Atlantic.

The other major impact on the jet scene during the late 1950s was made by the Sud-Aviation Caravelle, which entered service in May 1959 and was the pioneer of the 'clean' wing and rear-mounted engine layout. Numerically the Caravelle has not attained the sales record of the Boeing or Douglas jets, but it was a pace-setter when it first appeared and in its latest forms remains one of the world's leading jetliner types. For several years Sud-Aviation ran a highly successful sales campaign with the slogan *'Oh! Ils ont copié Caravelle!'*, and the proof of this statement can be seen in over a score of other designs, large and small and of many nationalities, now flying.

The aft-engine vogue has brought forth, in the second generation of jet transports, designs with two, three and four engines mounted in this fashion at or in the rear of the fuselage. The principal twin-engined types are the BAC One-Eleven and the McDonnell Douglas DC-9, both selling well according to their respective standards. The tri-jet formula is exemplified by the British Trident, Russia's Tu-154 and the American Boeing 727. The British story, unfortunately, is the all too familiar one of disappointing sales after being first in the field, while at the opposite extreme the Boeing 727 has proved to be the fastest-selling jet airliner in history. No American producer of a four-engined jet type has used the rear-engine formula, preferring the established underwing pod configuration instead; thus the only two exponents in this class are the VC10 and the Russian Il-62.

With the gradual improvement of the by-pass turbojet, or turbofan as it is more commonly called, there has been an increasing tendency to use this form of powerplant in preference to the turbojet, both in airliners and in smaller types of aircraft. Many of the established turbojet designs are available with, or have been converted to, fan engines, and an increasing number of newcomers are using this type of powerplant from the outset. First into service with a turbofan design was the Soviet Union with the Tu-124, a descendant of the Tu-104 already mentioned. Russia has also used turbofans in her supersonic transport, the Tu-144.

The most radical step in recent years in the field of subsonic jet transports was Boeing's decision to go ahead with what was quickly named the 'jumbo jet', the Boeing 747. More of a mammoth than a mere elephant, the 747 is designed to carry up to 490 people in an interior with 10-abreast seating whose proportions are more akin to a theatre auditorium than an airliner. Initial scepticism of whether there was really a need for an aeroplane of such a size seems to have been more than answered by the size of the order book and the traffic statistics during its first year and a half of operation. The 747 is, indeed, only the first of a new generation of wide-bodied airliners that will be flying the world's air routes in the 1970s. It was followed in 1971 by the McDonnell Douglas DC-10, and will in due course be joined also by the Lockheed TriStar, the A300B European Airbus and the smaller, shorter-range Dassault Mercure.

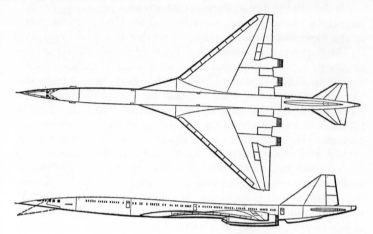

Anglo/French Concorde

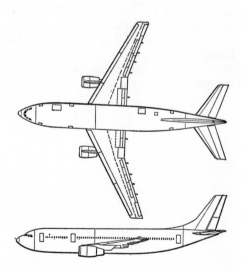

A300 B Airbus

Big though the 747 is, Boeing went out on an even longer limb financially when its design was chosen as the United States' entry in the supersonic airliner stakes. The other two world entrants, the Anglo/French Concorde and Russia's Tupolev Tu-144, are similar in basic concept and based on relatively straightforward airframes. Both are designed for similar supersonic speeds, the Concorde using turbojet engines and the Tu-144 turbofans. The initial Boeing SST submission, by comparison, was more complex by virtue of its adoption of the variable-geometry or 'swing-wing' concept. The complexity of this design led to its eventual withdrawal and replacement by the more conventional fixed-wing Boeing 2707-300, which itself fell victim to the 'environmentalist' lobby of American politics and was cancelled by the US Senate in March 1971. It is impossible to believe that America will not, eventually, build a supersonic transport aircraft; but when, and of what form, only the future will tell.

Perhaps it is not altogether irrelevant to conclude with a reference to an aeroplane at almost the opposite end of the speed spectrum to the SST: the perennial DC-3. With less than a quarter of the capacity and little more than a tenth of the speed of the Concorde this ageless, seemingly irreplaceable aeroplane has an unrivalled record in airline service stretching back over thirty-five of aviation's sixty-nine years. More than eight hundred DC-3's are still operational with over two hundred of the world's airlines: how many Concordes, one wonders, will still be in service thirty-five years from now?

THE COLOUR PLATES

As an aid to identification, the seventy-eight colour plates which follow have been arranged mainly on a visual basis, divided according to whether the aeroplane is propeller-driven or jet-driven and arranged in ascending order of the number of engines installed. The 'split' plan view technique is adopted to give, within a single plan outline, upper and lower surface markings of whichever aspect is represented by the side view.

The reference number of each aircraft corresponds to the appropriate text matter. An index to all types appears on p. 171.

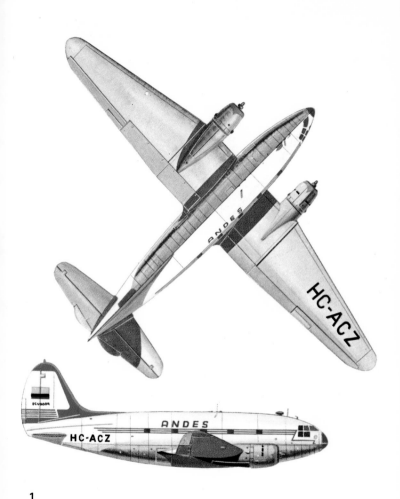

1

Curtiss C-46 of Lineas Aéreas Andes S.A., *ca* 1965. *Engines:* Two 2,000 h.p. Pratt & Whitney R-2800-51M1 Double Wasp eighteen-cylinder radial engines. *Span:* 108 ft. 0 in. (32·92 m.). *Length:* 76 ft. 4 in. (23·26 m.). *Wing area:* 1,358·0 sq. ft. (126·16 sq. m.). *Maximum take-off weight:* 48,000 lb. (21,772 kg.). *Typical cruising speed:* 195 m.p.h. (314 km/hr.) at 9,000 ft. (2,750 m.). *Service ceiling:* 24,500 ft. (7,470 m). *Range with payload of 9,584 lb. (4,347 kg.):* 1,800 miles (2,897 km.).

Il-14 (U.S.S.R.)

2

Avia 14 Salon (Czech-built Ilyushin Il-14) of Air Guinée, *ca* 1963. *Engines:*
Two 1,900 h.p. Shvetsov ASh–82T fourteen-cylinder radial engines. *Span:*
106 ft. 8 in. (32·41 m.). *Length:* 73 ft. 2 in. (22·30 m.). *Wing area:* 1,076·4
sq. ft. (100·00 sq. m.). *Maximum take-off weight:* 39,683 lb. (18,000 kg.).
Typical cruising speed: 186 m.p.h. (299 km/hr.) at 6,500 ft. (1,980 m.). *Service
ceiling:* 22,000 ft. (6,700 m.). *Range with maximum payload of 8,620 lb.
(3,910 kg.):* 280 miles (450 km.).

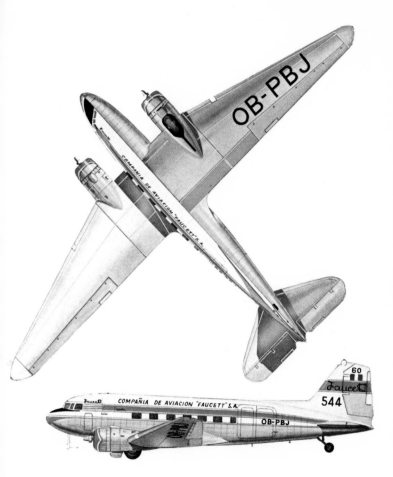

3

Douglas DC–3 of Compania de Aviacion Faucett S.A., *ca* 1965. *Engines:* Two 1,200 h.p. Pratt & Whitney R–1830–92 Twin Wasp fourteen-cylinder radial engines. *Span:* 95 ft. 0 in. (28·96 m.). *Length:* 64 ft. 0½ in. (19·52 m.). *Wing area:* 987·0 sq. ft. (91·70 sq. m.). *Maximum take-off weight:* 25,200 lb. (11,431 kg.). *Typical cruising speed:* 178 m.p.h. (286 km/hr.) at 10,000 ft. (3,050 m.). *Service ceiling:* 24,000 ft. (7,300 m). *Range with maximum payload of 5,000 lb. (2,268 kg.):* 660 miles (1,062 km.).

VIKING (U.K.)

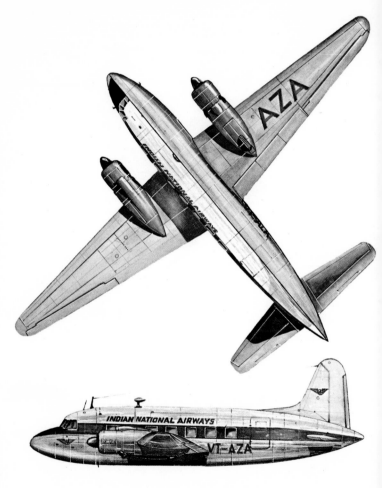

4

Vickers Type 604 Viking 1B *Jumna* of Indian National Airways, *ca* 1950. *Engines:* Two 1,690 h.p. Bristol Hercules 634 fourteen-cylinder radial engines. *Span:* 89 ft. 3 in. (27·20 m.). *Length:* 65 ft. 2 in. (19·86 m.). *Wing area:* 882·0 sq. ft. (81·94 sq. m.). *Maximum take-off weight:* 34,000 lb. (15,422 kg.). *Maximum cruising speed:* 210 m.p.h. (338 km./hr.) at 6,000 ft. (1,830 m.). *Service ceiling:* 23,750 ft. (7,240 m.). *Range with maximum payload of 7,240 lb. (3,284 kg.):* 520 miles (837 km.).

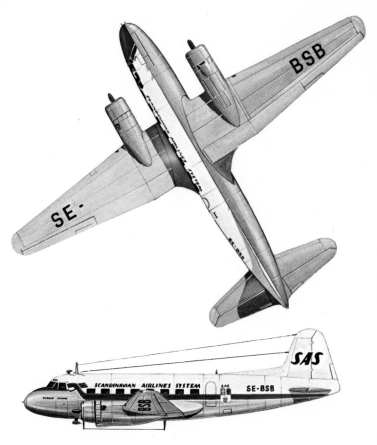

5

Saab 90A2 Scandia *Gardar Viking* of Scandinavian Airlines System, *ca* 1955
Engines: Two 1,800 h.p. Pratt & Whitney R–2180–E1 Twin Wasp eighteen-
cylinder radial engines. *Span:* 91 ft. 10¼ in. (28·00 m.). *Length:* 69 ft. 10½ in.
(21·30 m.). *Wing area:* 922·5 sq. ft. (85·70 sq. m.). *Maximum take-off weight:*
35,274 lb. (16,000 kg.). *Maximum cruising speed:* 242 m.p.h. (391 km/hr.) at
10,000 ft. (3,050 m.). *Service ceiling:* 22,850 ft. (7,500 m.). *Range with
6,173 lb. (2,800 kg.) payload:* 920 miles (1,480 km.).

AMBASSADOR (U.K.)

6
Airspeed A.S.57 Ambassador Srs. 2 of Dan-Air Services Ltd., *ca* 1967. *Engines:* Two 2,625 h.p. Bristol Centaurus 661 eighteen-cylinder radial engines. *Span:* 115 ft. 0 in. (35·05 m.). *Length:* 82 ft. 0 in. (24·99 m.). *Wing area:* 1,200·0 sq. ft. (111·48 sq. m.). *Maximum take-off weight:* 55,000 lb. (24,948 kg.). *Typical cruising speed:* 240 m.p.h. (386 km/hr.) at 15,000 ft. (4,570 m.). *Range with maximum payload of 10,800 lb. (4,900 kg.):* 445 miles (716 km.).

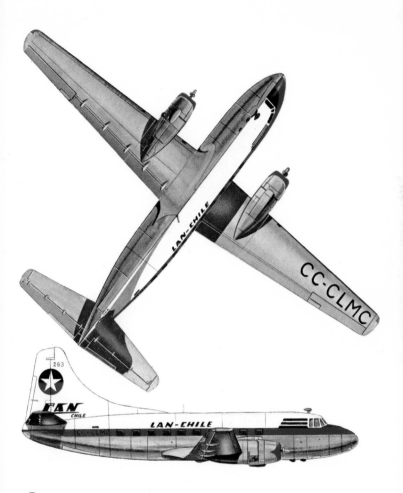

7

Martin 2–0–2 of Linea Aérea Nacional de Chile (LAN-Chile), *ca* 1948/49. *Engines:* Two 2,400 h.p. Pratt & Whitney R–2800–CA18 Double Wasp eighteen-cylinder radial engines. *Span:* 93 ft. 3 in. (28·42 m.). *Length:* 71 ft. 4 in. (21·74 m.). *Wing area:* 864·0 sq. ft. (80·27 sq. m.). *Maximum take-off weight:* 39,900 lb. (18,098 kg.). *Typical cruising speed:* 286 m.p.h. (460 km/hr.) at 12,000 ft. (3,660 m.). *Service ceiling:* 33,000 ft. (10,060 m.). *Range with maximum payload of 9,270 lb. (4,205 kg.) and reserves:* 635 miles (1,022 km.).

CONVAIR 240 (U.S.A.)

8
Convair 240 of Ethiopian Airlines S.C., *ca* 1959/60. *Engines:* Two 2,400 h.p. Pratt & Whitney R–2800–CA18 Double Wasp eighteen-cylinder radial engines. *Span:* 91 ft. 9 in. (27·96 m.). *Length:* 74 ft. 8 in. (22·76 m.). *Wing area:* 817·0 sq. ft. (75·90 sq. m.). *Maximum take-off weight:* 41,790 lb. (18,955 kg.). *Typical cruising speed:* 235 m.p.h. (378 km/hr.) at 8,000 ft. (2,440 m.). *Service ceiling:* 30,000 ft. (9,150 m.). *Range with maximum payload of 9,250 lb. (4,195 kg.):* 690 miles (1,110 km.).

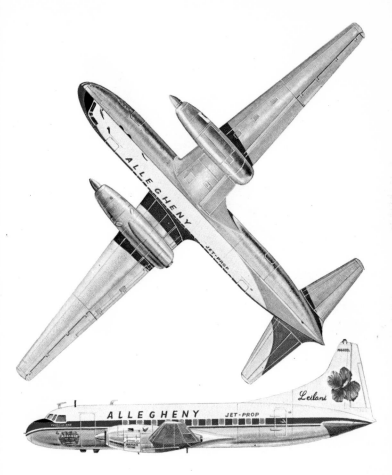

9

Convair 540 (ex-340) leased to Allegheny Airlines Inc. in July 1959 for experimental services. *Engines:* Two 3,500 e.h.p. Napier Eland 504A turboprops. *Span:* 105 ft. 4 in. (32·10 m.). *Length:* 79 ft. 2 in. (24·57 m.). *Wing area:* 920·0 sq. ft. (85·47 sq. m.). *Maximum take-off weight:* 53,200 lb. (24,131 kg.). *Maximum cruising speed:* 325 m.p.h. (523 km/hr.) at 20,000 ft. (6,100 m.). *Service ceiling:* 21,000 ft. (6,400 m.). *Range with maximum payload of 12,986 lb. (5,890 kg.):* 905 miles (1,456 km.).

NAMC YS-11 (Japan)

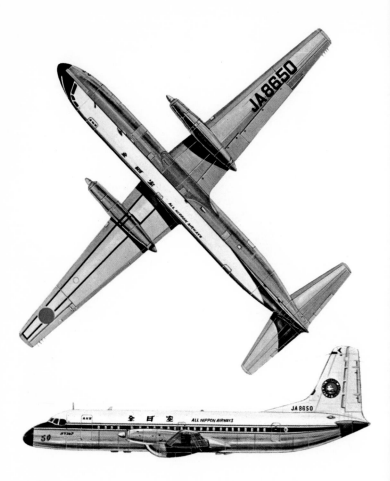

10

NAMC YS–11–102 of All Nippon Airways Co., *ca* 1966. *Engines:* Two 3,060 e.h.p. Rolls-Royce Dart Mk.542–10 turboprops. *Span:* 104 ft. 11¾ in. (32·00 m.). *Length:* 86 ft. 3½ in. (26·30 m.). *Wing area:* 1,020·4 sq. ft. (94·80 sq. m.). *Maximum take-off weight:* 51,808 lb. (23,500 kg.). *Maximum cruising speed:* 297 m.p.h. (478 km/hr.) at 15,000 ft. (4,575 m.). *Service ceiling:* 27,500 ft. (8,380 m.). *Range with maximum payload of 12,350 lb. (5,600 kg.):* 860 miles (1,390 km.).

11
Hawker Siddeley 748 Srs. 2 of Air Ceylon Ltd., *ca* 1965. *Engines:* Two 2,105
e.s.h.p. Rolls-Royce Dart Mk. 531 turboprops. *Span:* 98 ft. 6 in. (30·02 m.).
Length: 67 ft. 0 in. (20·42 m.). *Wing area:* 810·75 sq. ft. (75·35 sq. m.).
Maximum take-off weight: 44,495 lb. (20,182 kg.). *Maximum cruising speed:*
287 m.p.h. (462 km/hr.) at 15,000 ft. (4,570 m.). *Service ceiling:* 25,000 ft.
(7,620 m.). *Range with maximum payload of 11,512 lb. (5,221 kg.):* 690 miles
(1,110 km.).

FRIENDSHIP (Netherlands)

12

Fairchild Hiller F-27A of Bonanza Air Lines Inc., *ca* 1959. *Engines:* Two 2,050 e.h.p. Rolls-Royce Dart Mk.528–7E turboprops. *Span:* 95 ft. 2 in. (29·00 m.). *Length:* 77 ft. 2 in. (23·50 m.). *Wing area:* 753·5 sq. ft. (70·00 sq. m.). *Maximum take-off weight:* 42,000 lb. (19,050 kg.). *Maximum cruising speed:* 300 m.p.h. (483 km/hr.) at 20,000 ft. (6,100 m.). *Service ceiling:* 32,600 ft. (9,935 m.). *Range with maximum payload of 12,500 lb. (5,670 kg.):* 912 miles (1,468 km.).

13

Antonov An–24V Series I of Transporturile Aeriene Romine (Tarom), *ca* 1967. *Engines:* Two 2,550 e.h.p. Ivchenko AI–24 turboprops. *Span:* 95 ft. $9\frac{1}{2}$ in. (29·20 m.). *Length:* 77 ft. $2\frac{1}{2}$ in. (23·53 m.). *Wing area:* 780·0 sq. ft. (72·46 sq. m.). *Maximum take-off weight:* 46,300 lb. (21,000 kg.). *Maximum cruising speed:* 310 m.p.h. (500 km/hr.) at 19,700 ft. (6,000 m.). *Service ceiling:* 29,500 ft. (9,000 m.). *Range with maximum payload of 12,565 lb. (5,700 kg.):* 404 miles (650 km.).

HERALD (U.K.)

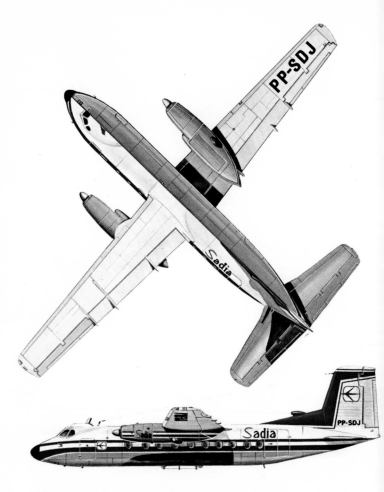

14

Handley Page H.P.R.7 Herald 214 of Sadia S.A. Transportes Aéreos, *ca* 1966. *Engines:* Two 2,105 e.h.p. Rolls-Royce Dart Mk.527 turboprops. *Span:* 94 ft. 9 in. (28·88 m.). *Length:* 75 ft. 6 in. (23·01 m.). *Wing area:* 886·0 sq. ft. (82·31 sq. m.). *Maximum take-off weight:* 43,000 lb. (19,500 kg.). *Maximum cruising speed:* 275 m.p.h. (443 km/hr.) at 15,000 ft. (4,575 m.). *Service ceiling:* 27,900 ft. (8,500 m.). *Range with maximum payload of 11,242 lb. (5,100 kg.):* 700 miles (1,125 km.).

AÉROSPATIALE N 262 (France)

15

Aérospatiale N 262 Series A of Japan Domestic Airlines (Nippon Kokunai Koku), *ca* 1966. *Engines:* Two 1,065 e.s.h.p. Turboméca Bastan VIC turbo-props. *Span:* 71 ft. 10 in. (21·90 m.). *Length:* 63 ft. 3 in. (19·28 m.). *Wing area:* 592·0 sq. ft. (55·00 sq. m.). *Maximum take-off weight:* 22,930 lb. (10,400 kg.). *Maximum cruising speed:* 233 m.p.h. (375 km/hr.) at 15,000 ft. (4,570 m.). *Service ceiling:* 19,200 ft. (5,850 m.). *Range with maximum payload of 7,280 lb. (3,302 kg.):* 545 miles (875 km.).

SAUNDERS ST-27 (Canada)

16

Saunders ST–27 in manufacturer's demonstration livery, 1971. *Engines:* Two 715 e.s.h.p. Pratt & Whitney (UACL) PT6A–27 turboprops. *Span:* 71 ft. 6 in. (21·79 m.). *Length:* 58 ft. 10 in. (17·93 m.). *Wing area:* 499·0 sq. ft. (46·36 sq. m.). *Maximum take-off weight:* 13,500 lb. (6,124 kg.). *Maximum cruising speed:* 230 m.p.h. (370 km/hr.) at 7,000 ft. (2,135 m.). *Service ceiling:* 25,000 ft. (7,620 m.). *Maximum range:* 852 miles (1,370 km.).

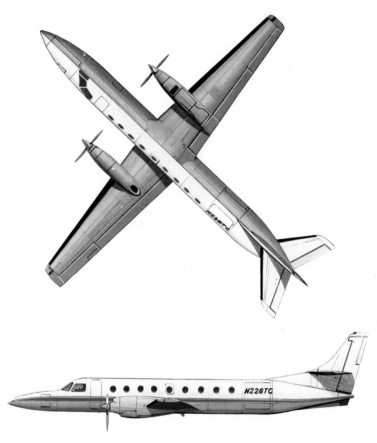

17

Swearingen SA–226TC Metro prototype in manufacturer's demonstration livery, 1970. *Engines:* Two 940 s.h.p. AiResearch TPE 331–3U–303 turbo-props. *Span:* 46 ft. 3 in. (14·10 m.). *Length:* 59 ft. 4¼ in. (18·09 m.). *Wing area:* 277·5 sq. ft. (25·78 sq. m.). *Maximum take-off weight:* 12,500 lb. (5,670 kg.). *Maximum cruising speed:* 290 m.p.h. (467 km/hr.) at 10,500 ft. (3,050 m.). *Typical range with 3,965 lb. (1,798 kg.) payload:* 345 miles (555 km.).

TURBOLET (Czechoslovakia)

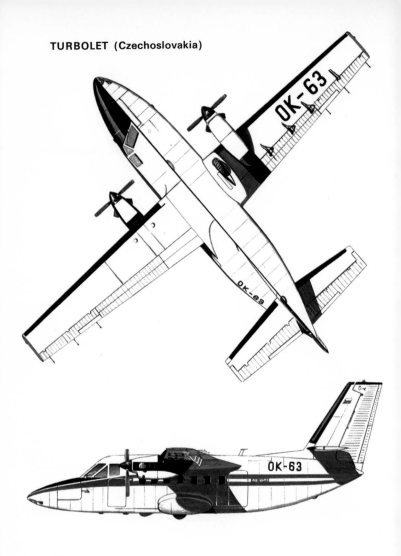

18

Let L–410 Turbolet, prototype aircraft in manufacturer's demonstration livery, 1970. *Engines:* Two 715 e.s.h.p. Pratt & Whitney (UACL) PT6A–27 turbo-props. *Span:* 56 ft. 1½ in. (17·10 m.). *Length:* 44 ft. 7¾ in. (13·61 m.). *Wing area:* 349·8 sq. ft. (32·50 sq. m.). *Maximum take-off weight:* 11,245 lb. (5,100 kg.). *Maximum cruising speed:* 229 m.p.h. (369 km/hr.) at 9,850 ft. (3,000 m.). *Service ceiling:* 25,500 ft. (7,770 m.). *Maximum range:* 705 miles (1,140 km.).

19

de Havilland Canada DHC–6 Twin Otter Series 100 of Trans-Australia Airlines, 1967. *Engines:* Two 579 e.s.h.p. Pratt & Whitney (UACL) PT6A–20 turbo-props. *Span:* 65 ft. 0 in. (19·81 m.). *Length:* 49 ft. 6 in. (15·09 m.). *Wing area:* 420·0 sq. ft. (39·02 sq. m.). *Maximum take-off weight:* 11,579 lb. (5,252 kg.). *Maximum cruising speed:* 184 m.p.h. (297 km/hr.) at 10,000 ft. (3,050 m.). *Service ceiling:* 25,500 ft. (7,770 m.). *Maximum range:* 920 miles (1,480 km.).

Ju 52/3m (Germany)

20

Junkers Ju 52/3m *Karjala* of Aero O/Y (Finnair), *ca* 1947. *Engines:* Three 770 h.p. BMW 132H nine-cylinder radial engines. *Span:* 95 ft. 11½ in. (29·25 m.). *Length:* 62 ft. 0 in. (18·90 m.). *Wing area:* 1,189·4 sq. ft. (110·50 sq. m.). *Maximum take-off weight:* 23,150 lb. (10,500 kg.). *Typical cruising speed:* 154 m.p.h. (248 km/hr.) at 8,200 ft. (2,500 m.). *Service ceiling:* 19,025 ft. (5,800 m.). *Typical range:* 545 miles (880 km.).

21

Britten-Norman BN–2A Mk III Trislander of Aurigny Air Services, 1971.
Engines: Three 260 h.p. Lycoming O–540–E4C5 six-cylinder horizontally-opposed type. *Span:* 53 ft. 0 in. (16·15 m.). *Length:* 43 ft. 9 in. (13·335 m.).
Wing area: 337·0 sq. ft. (31·31 sq. m.). *Maximum take-off weight:* 9,350 lb.
(4,241 kg.). *Maximum cruising speed:* 180 m.p.h. (290 km/hr.) at 6,500 ft.
(1,980 m.). *Service ceiling:* 14,500 ft. (4,420 m.). *Maximum range:* 1,000 miles
(1,610 km.).

LANCASTRIAN (U.K.)

22

Avro 691 Lancastrian 1 *Nepal* of British Overseas Airways Corporation, *ca* 1948. *Engines:* Four 1,635 h.p. Rolls-Royce Merlin T.24/4 twelve-cylinder Vee-type engines. *Span:* 102 ft. 0 in. (31·09 m.). *Length:* 76 ft. 10 in. (23·42 m.). *Wing area:* 1,297·0 sq. ft. (119·49 sq. m.). *Maximum take-off weight:* 65,000 lb. (29,484 kg.). *Typical cruising speed:* 280 m.p.h. (451 km/hr.) at 11,000 ft. (3,350 m.). *Service ceiling:* 24,300 ft. (7,400 m.). *Range with maximum fuel:* 2,820 miles (4,540 km.).

23

Handley Page H.P.70 Halton 2 operated by British American Air Services Ltd. in 1946 on behalf of The Maharajah Gaekwar of Baroda. *Engines:* Four 1,675 h.p. Bristol Hercules 100 fourteen-cylinder radial engines. *Span:* 103 ft. 8 in. (31·59 m.). *Length:* 73 ft. 7 in. (22·43 m.). *Wing area:* 1,278·0 sq. ft. (118·73 sq. m.). *Maximum take-off weight:* 68,000 lb. (30,844 kg.). *Maximum cruising speed:* 260 m.p.h. (418 km/hr.) at 15,000 ft. (4,570 m.). *Service ceiling:* 21,000 ft. (6,400 m.). *Range with maximum payload of 8,000 lb. (3,629 kg.):* 2,530 miles (4,072 km.).

24

Bristol 167 Brabazon 1 prototype, *ca* 1950. *Engines:* Eight 2,500 h.p. Bristol Centaurus 20 eighteen-cylinder radial engines. *Span:* 230 ft. 0 in. (70·10 m.). *Length:* 177 ft. 0 in. (53·95 m.). *Wing area:* 5,317·0 sq. ft. (493·97 sq. m.). *Maximum take-off weight:* 290,000 lb. (131,540 kg.). *Maximum cruising speed:* 250 m.p.h. (402 km/hr.) at 25,000 ft. (7,620 m.). *Range with maximum fuel:* 5,500 miles (8,851 km.).

TUDOR (U.K.)

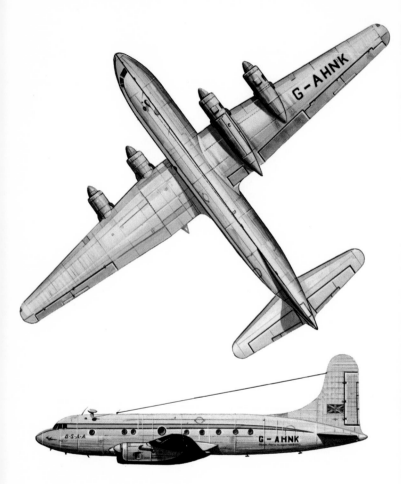

25

Avro 688 Tudor 4 *Star Lion* of British South American Airways, *ca* 1948.
Engines: Four 1,770 h.p. Rolls-Royce Merlin 621 twelve-cylinder Vee-type
engines. *Span:* 120 ft. 0 in. (36·58 m.). *Length:* 85 ft. 3 in. (25·98 m.). *Wing
area:* 1,421·0 sq. ft. (132·01 sq. m.). *Maximum take-off weight:* 80,000 lb.
(36,287 kg.). *Maximum cruising speed:* 210 m.p.h. (338 km/hr.) at 20,000 ft.
(6,100 m.). *Service ceiling:* 27,400 ft. (8,350 m.). *Range with maximum fuel:*
4,000 miles (6,437 km.).

26

Handley Page H.P.81 Hermes 4A of Airwork Ltd, *ca* 1953. *Engines:* Four 2,125 h.p. Bristol Hercules 773 fourteen-cylinder radial engines. *Span:* 113 ft. 0 in. (34·44 m.). *Length:* 96 ft. 10 in. (29·51 m.). *Wing area:* 1,408·0 sq. ft. (130·80 sq. m.). *Maximum take-off weight:* 86,000 lb. (39,009 kg.). *Maximum cruising speed:* 270 m.p.h. (435 km/hr.) at 20,000 ft. (6,100 m.). *Service ceiling:* 23,800 ft. (7,250 m.). *Range with payload of 14,125 lb. (6,407 kg.):* 2,000 miles (3,219 km.).

STRATOCRUISER (U.S.A.)

27

Boeing 377–10–26 Stratocruiser *Clipper Washington* of Pan American World Airways Inc, *ca* 1951. *Engines:* Four 3,500 h.p. Pratt & Whitney R–4360–B6 Wasp Major twenty-eight-cylinder radial engines. *Span:* 141 ft. 3 in. (43·05 m.). *Length:* 110 ft. 4 in. (33·63 m.). *Wing area:* 1,769·0 sq. ft. (164·35 sq. m.). *Maximum take-off weight:* 142,500 lb. (64,634 kg.). *Maximum cruising speed:* 340 m.p.h. (547 km/hr.) at 25,000 ft. (7,620 m.). *Service ceiling:* 33,000 ft. (10,000 m.). *Range with maximum payload of 23,930 lb. (10,855 kg.):* 2,750 miles (4,426 km.).

DOUGLAS DC-4 (U.S.A.)

28

Douglas DC–4 of Linea Expresa Bolivar C.A. (LEBCA), *ca 1963. Engines:* Four 1,450 h.p. Pratt & Whitney R–2000–SD13G Twin Wasp fourteen-cylinder radial engines. *Span:* 117 ft. 6 in. (35·80 m.). *Length:* 93 ft. 11 in. (28·63 m.). *Wing area:* 1,463·0 sq. ft. (136·91 sq. m.). *Maximum take-off weight:* 73,000 lb. (33,112 kg.). *Typical cruising speed:* 227 m.p.h. (365 km/hr.) at 10,000 ft. (3,050 m.). *Service ceiling:* 22,300 ft. (6,800 m.). *Range with maximum payload of 12,700 lb. (5,760 kg.):* 2,140 miles (3,444 km.).

DOUGLAS DC-6 (U.S.A.)

29

Douglas DC–6B of Hawaiian Airlines Inc, *ca* 1965. *Engines:* Four 2,500 h.p.
Pratt & Whitney R–2800–CB17 Double Wasp eighteen-cylinder radial engines.
Span: 117 ft. 6 in. (35·80 m.). *Length:* 106 ft. 8 in. (32·50 m.). *Wing area:*
1,463·0 sq. ft. (136·91 sq. m.). *Maximum take-off weight;* 106,000 lb. (48,081
kg.). *Typical cruising speed:* 311 m.p.h. (500 km/hr.) at 22,500 ft. (6,860 m.).
Service ceiling: 25,000 ft. (7,620 m.). *Range with maximum payload of 19,200
lb. (8,709 kg.):* 3,050 miles (4,908 km.).

DOUGLAS DC-7 (U.S.A.)

30

Douglas DC–7F *Irish Sea* of Koninklijke Luchtvaart Maatschappij N.V. (K.L.M. Royal Dutch Airlines), *ca* 1963. *Engines:* Four 3,400 h.p. Wright R–3350–988TC–18EA–4 eighteen-cylinder Turbo Compound radial engines. *Span:* 127 ft. 6 in. (38·86 m.). *Length:* 112 ft. 3 in. (34·21 m.). *Wing area:* 1,637·0 sq. ft. (152·08 sq. m.). *Maximum take-off weight:* 143,000 lb. (64,863 kg.). *Typical cruising speed:* 360 m.p.h. (579 km/hr.) at 23,500 ft. (7,165 m.). *Service ceiling:* 25,000 ft. (7,620 m.). *Range with maximum payload of 35,275 lb. (16 000 kg.):* 4,250 miles (6,840 km.).

S.M. 95 (Italy)

31

SIAI-Marchetti S.M.95 *Cristoforo Colombo* of Alitalia, *ca* 1948. *Engines:* Four 850 h.p. Alfa Romeo 128 RC 18 nine-cylinder radial engines. *Span:* 112 ft. 5$\frac{1}{4}$ in. (34·28 m.). *Length:* 81 ft. 3$\frac{1}{4}$ in. (24·77 m.). *Wing area:* 1,381·0 sq. ft. (128·30 sq. m.). *Maximum take-off weight:* 47,642 lb. (21,610 kg.). *Typical cruising speed:* 196 m.p.h. (315 km/hr.) at 11,480 ft. (3,500 m.). *Service ceiling:* 20,830 ft. (6,350 m.). *Range with payload of 8,977 lb. (4,072 kg.):* 1,242 miles (2,000 km.).

32

Sud-Est S.E.161 Languedoç of Polskie Linie Lotnicze (LOT), *ca* 1948. *Engines:* Four 1,200 h.p. Gnome-Rhône 14N 68/69 fourteen-cylinder radial engines. *Span:* 96 ft. 4¾ in. (29·38 m.). *Length:* 79 ft. 6¾ in. (24·25 m.). *Wing area:* 1,198·0 sq. ft. (111·30 sq. m.). *Maximum take-off weight:* 50,576 lb. (22,940 kg.). *Typical cruising speed:* 252 m.p.h. (405 km/hr.) at 10,825 ft. (3,300 m.). *Service ceiling:* 23,625 ft. (7,200 m.). *Range with maximum payload of 8,752 lb. (3,970 kg.):* 620 miles (1,000 km.).

MARATHON (U.K.)

33

Handley Page H.P.R.1 Marathon 1A *Lagos* of West African Airways Corporation, *ca* 1952. *Engines:* Four 340 h.p. de Havilland Gipsy Queen 70 Mk. 4 six-cylinder inline engines. *Span:* 65 ft. 0 in. (19·81 m.). *Length:* 52 ft. 1½ in. (15·88 m.). *Wing area:* 498·0 sq. ft. (46·26 sq. m.). *Maximum take-off weight:* 18,250 lb. (8,278 kg.). *Maximum cruising speed:* 201 m.p.h. (324 km/hr.) at 10,000 ft. (3,050 m.). *Service ceiling:* 18,000 ft. (5,490 m.). *Range with payload of 4,172 lb. (1,892 kg.):* 720 miles (1,160 km.).

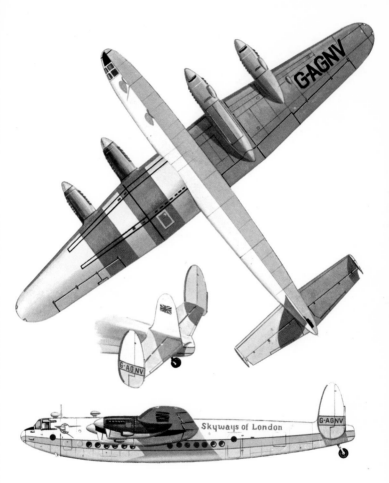

34

Avro 685 York 1 of Skyways Ltd, *ca* 1955. *Engines:* Four 1,610 h.p. Rolls-Royce Merlin 502 twelve-cylinder Vee-type engines. *Span:* 102 ft. 0 in. (31·09 m.). *Length:* 78 ft. 6 in. (23·92 m.). *Wing area:* 1,297·0 sq. ft. (119·49 sq. m.). *Maximum take-off weight:* 70,000 lb. (31,751 kg.). *Typical cruising speed:* 210 m.p.h. (338 km/hr.) at 10,000 ft. (3,050 m.). *Service ceiling:* 23,000 ft. (7,010 m.). *Range with maximum payload of 20,000 lb. (9,072 kg.):* 1,400 miles (2,253 km.).

CONSTELLATION (U.S.A.)

35

Lockheed Model 049 Constellation *Paris Sky Chief* of Trans World Airline, *ca* 1946. *Engines:* Four 2,200 h.p. Wright R–3350–C18–BA–1 Cyclone 18 eighteen-cylinder radial engines. *Span:* 123 ft. 0 in. (37·49 m.). *Length:* 95 ft. 2 in. (29·00 m.). *Wing area:* 1,650·0 sq. ft. (153·28 sq. m.). *Maximum take-off weight:* 86,250 lb. (39,112 kg.). *Typical cruising speed:* 313 m.p.h. (504 km/hr.) at 20,000 ft. (6,100 m.). *Service ceiling:* 25,000 ft. (7,620 m.). *Typical range:* 3,050 miles (4,908 km.).

SUPER CONSTELLATION (U.S.A.)

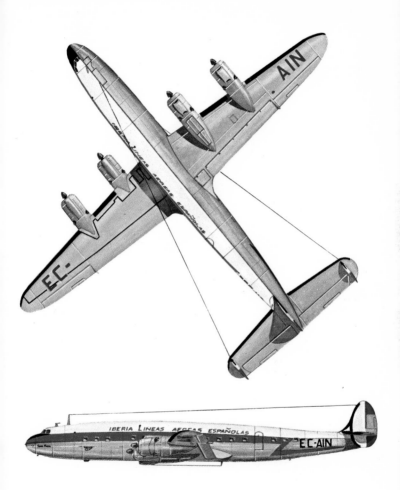

36

Lockheed Model L.1049E Super Constellation *Santa Maria* of Lineas Aéreas
Españolas S.A. (Iberia), *ca* 1955. *Engines:* Four 3,250 h.p. Wright R−3350−
C18−DA−1 Turbo Compounds. *Span:* 123 ft. 0 in. (37·49 m.). *Length:* 113 ft.
7 in. (34·65 m.). *Wing area:* 1,650·0 sq. ft. (153·28 sq. m.). *Maximum take-off
weight:* 150,000 lb. (68,100 kg.). *Maximum cruising speed:* 327 m.p.h. (523
km/hr.) at 20,000 ft. (6,100 m.). *Service ceiling:* 25,000 ft. (7,620 m.). *Range
with maximum payload of 26,400 lb. (11,974 kg.):* 3,100 miles (4,990 km.).

VISCOUNT 700 (U.K.)

37

Vickers Viscount 779 of Fred. Olsen Air Transport Ltd, *ca* 1957. *Engines:* Four 1,740 e.h.p. Rolls-Royce Dart Mk.510 turboprops. *Span:* 93 ft. 8½ in. (28·56 m.). *Length:* 81 ft. 10 in. (25·04 m.). *Wing area:* 963·0 sq. ft. (89·47 sq. m). *Maximum take-off weight:* 64,500 lb. (29,257 kg.). *Maximum cruising speed:* 334 m.p.h. (537 km/hr.) at 20,000 ft. (6,100 m.). *Service ceiling:* 27,500 ft. (8,380 m.). *Range with maximum payload of 11,842 lb. (5,372 kg.):* 1,748 miles (2,813 km.).

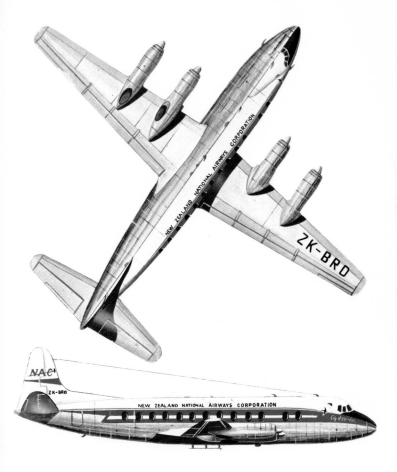

38

Vickers Viscount 807 *City of Wellington* of New Zealand National Airways Corporation, *ca* 1959. *Engines:* Four 1,740 e.h.p. Rolls-Royce Dart Mk. 510 turboprops. *Span:* 93 ft. 8½ in. (28·56 m.). *Length:* 85 ft. 8 in. (26·11 m.). *Wing area:* 963·0 sq. ft. (89·47 sq. m.). *Maximum take-off weight:* 64,500 lb. (29,257 kg.). *Typical cruising speed:* 305 m.p.h. (491 km/hr.) at 19,500 ft. (5,950 m.). *Service ceiling:* 27,000 ft. (8,230 m.). *Range with maximum payload of 12,900 lb. (5,851 kg.):* 1,290 miles (2,075 km.).

PROVENCE (France)

39

Breguet Br.763 Provence of Compagnie Nationale Air France, *ca* 1953. *Engines:* Four 2,400 h.p. Pratt & Whitney R–2800–CA18 Double Wasp eighteen-cylinder radial engines. *Span:* 141 ft. $0\frac{1}{2}$ in. (42·99 m.). *Length:* 94 ft. $11\frac{1}{2}$ in. (28·94 m.). *Wing area:* 1,995·6 sq. ft. (185·40 sq. m.). *Maximum take-off weight:* 113,759 lb. (51,600 kg.). *Typical cruising speed:* 218 m.p.h. (351 km/hr.) at 10,000 ft. (3,050 m.). *Service ceiling:* 24,000 ft. (7,300 m.). *Typical range with maximum payload of 26,960 lb. (12,228 kg.):* 1,345 miles (2,165 km.).

40

Aviation Traders ATL.98 Carvair *St Jarlaith* of Aer Lingus Teoranta, *ca* 1964.
Engines: Four 1,450 h.p. Pratt & Whitney R–2000–7M2 Twin Wasp fourteen-
cylinder radials. *Span:* 117 ft. 6 in. (35·82 m.). *Length:* 102 ft. 7 in. (31·27 m.).
Wing area: 1,462·0 sq. ft. (135·82 sq. m.). *Maximum take-off weight:* 73,800 lb.
(33,475 kg.). *Maximum cruising speed:* 213 m.p.h. (342 km/hr.) at 10,000 ft.
(3,050 m.). *Service ceiling:* 18,700 ft. (5,700 m.). *Range with maximum payload
of 17,635 lb. (8,000 kg.):* 2,300 miles (3,700 km.).

BRITANNIA (U.K.)

41

Bristol Britannia 312 *Justice* of British Eagle International Airlines Ltd, *ca* 1965.
Engines: Four 4,445 e.h.p. Bristol Siddeley Proteus 765 turboprops. *Span:*
142 ft. 3 in. (43·36 m.). *Length:* 124 ft. 3 in. (37·87 m.). *Wing area:* 2,075·0
sq. ft. (192·78 sq. m.). *Maximum take-off weight:* 185,000 lb. (83,914 kg.).
Maximum cruising speed: 402 m.p.h. (647 km/hr.) at 21,000 ft. (6,400 m.).
Service ceiling: 24,000 ft. (7,300 m.). *Range with maximum payload of
34,900 lb. (15,830 kg.):* 4,268 miles (6,870 km.).

42

Canadair CL–44D–4 of The Flying Tiger Line Inc, *ca* 1962. *Engines:* Four 5,730 e.s.h.p. Rolls-Royce Tyne Mk 515/10 turboprops. *Span:* 142 ft. 3⅜ in. (43·37 m.). *Length:* 136 ft. 8 in. (41·65 m.). *Wing area:* 2,075·0 sq. ft. (192·78 sq. m.). *Maximum take-off weight:* 210,000 lb. (95,250 kg.). *Typical cruising speed:* 316 m.p.h. (506 km/hr.) at 20,340 ft. (6,200 m.). *Service ceiling:* 30,000 ft. (9,145 m.). *Range with maximum payload of 63,272 lb. (28,725 kg.):* 2,875 miles (4,600 km.).

ELECTRA (U.S.A.)

43

Lockheed L–188C Electra *Aotearoa* of Air New Zealand Ltd, *ca* 1967. *Engines:*
Four 3,750 e.s.h.p. Allison 501–D13A turboprops. *Span:* 99 ft. 0 in. (30·18 m.).
Length: 104 ft. 8 in. (31·90 m.). *Wing area:* 1,300·0 sq. ft. (120·77 sq. m.).
Maximum take-off weight: 116,000 lb. (52,617 kg.). *Maximum cruising speed:*
405 m.p.h. (652 km/hr.) at 22,000 ft. (6,700 m.). *Service ceiling:* 27,000 ft.
(8,230 m.). *Range with 22,000 lb. (9,979 kg.) payload:* 2,500 miles (4,023 km.).

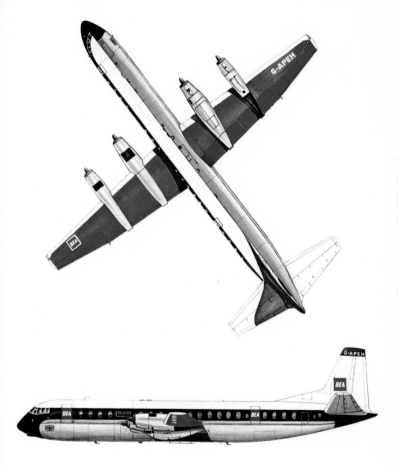

44

Vickers Vanguard 953 of British European Airways Corporation, *ca* 1966.
Engines: Four 4,985 e.h.p. Rolls-Royce Tyne Mk. 506 turboprops. *Span:*
118 ft. 0 in. (35·96 m.). *Length:* 122 ft. 10½ in. (37·38 m.). *Wing area:* 1,529·0
sq. ft. (142·04 sq. m.). *Maximum take-off weight:* 146,500 lb. (66,451 kg.).
Maximum cruising speed: 425 m.p.h. (680 km/hr.) at 20,000 ft. (6,100 m.).
Range with maximum payload of 37,000 lb. (16,783 kg.): 1,590 miles
(2,560 km.).

II-18 (U.S.S.R.)

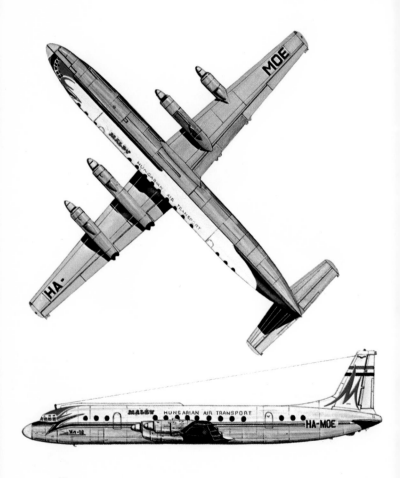

45
Ilyushin II—18V Moskva of Magyar Legiközlekedesi Vallalat (Malév), *ca* 1965.
Engines: Four 4,000 e.h.p. Ivchenko AI—20K turboprops.. *Span:* 122 ft. 8½ in.
(37·40 m.). *Length:* 117 ft. 9 in. (35·90 m.). *Wing area:* 1,506·95 sq. ft.
(140·00 sq. m.). *Maximum take-off weight:* 134,925 lb. (61,200 kg.). *Maximum
cruising speed:* 404 m.p.h. (650 km/hr.) at 29,500 ft. (9,000 m.). *Service ceiling:*
32,800 ft. (10,000 m.). *Range with maximum payload of 29,762 lb. (13,500
kg.):* 1,553 miles (2,500 km.).

46

Antonov An–10A of Aeroflot, *ca* 1960. *Engines:* Four 4,000 e.h.p. Ivchenko AI–20K turboprops. *Span:* 124 ft. 8 in. (38·0 m.). *Length:* 111 ft. 6½ in. (34·0 m.). *Wing area:* 1,291·7 sq. ft. (120·00 sq. m.). *Maximum take-off weight:* 121,500 lb. (55,100 kg.). *Maximum cruising speed:* 422 m.p.h. (680 km/hr.) at 32,800 ft. (10,000 m.). *Service ceiling:* 33,465 ft. (10,200 m.). *Range with maximum payload of 32,000 lb. (14,500 kg.):* 745 miles (1,200 km.).

Tu-114 (U.S.S.R.)

47

Tupelov Tu-114 of Aeroflot, *ca* 1961. *Engines:* Four 14,795 e.s.h.p. Kuznetsov NK-12MV turboprops. *Span:* 167 ft. 8 in. (51·10 m.). *Length:* 177 ft. 6 in. (54·10 m.). *Wing area:* 3,348·6 sq. ft. (311·10 sq. m.). *Maximum take-off weight:* 376,990 lb. (171,000 kg.). *Maximum cruising speed:* 478 m.p.h. (770 km/hr.) at 29,500 ft. (9,000 m.). *Service ceiling:* 39,370 ft. (12,000 m.). *Range with maximum payload of 66,140 lb. (30,000 kg.):* 3,850 miles (6,200 km.).

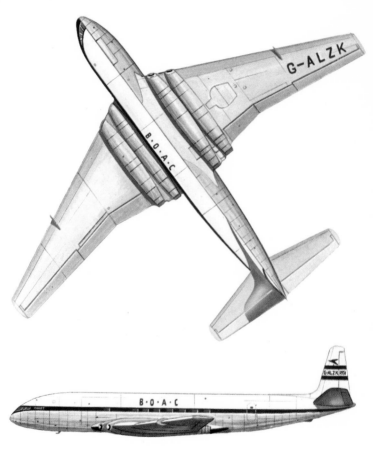

48

Second M.o.S. prototype for the de Havilland D.H.106 Comet 1 in the colours of British Overseas Airways Corporation, *ca* 1951. *Engines:* Four 4,450 lb. (2,018 kg.) s.t. de Havilland Ghost 50 Mk. 1 turbojets. *Span:* 115 ft. 0 in. (35·05 m.). *Length:* 93 ft. 1¼ in. (28·38 m.). *Wing area:* 2,015·0 sq. ft. (187·20 sq. m.). *Maximum take-off weight:* 105,000 lb. (47,627 kg.). *Maximum cruising speed:* 490 m.p.h. (788 km/hr.) at 35,000 ft. (10,700 m.). *Service ceiling:* 40,000 ft. (12,190 m.). *Range with maximum payload of 12,000 lb. (5,443 kg.):* 1,750 miles (2,816 km.).

Tu-104 (U.S.S.R.)

49

Tupolev Tu-104A *Brno* of Československé Aerolinie (CSA), *ca* 1958. *Engines:* Two 21,385 lb. (9,700 kg.) s.t. Mikulin AM−3M−500 turbojets. *Span:* 113 ft. 4 in. (34·54 m.). *Length:* 127 ft. 5½ in. (38·85 m.). *Wing area:* 1,877·2 sq. ft. (174·40 sq. m.). *Maximum take-off weight:* 167,550 lb. (76,000 kg.). *Maximum cruising speed:* 560 m.p.h. (900 km/hr.) at 32,800 ft. (10,000 m.). *Service ceiling:* 37,750 ft. (11,500 m.). *Range with maximum payload of 19,840 lb. (9,000 kg.):* 1,645 miles (2,650 km.).

50

Tupolev Tu-124V *Centrotex* of Československé Aerolinie (CSA), *ca* 1967.
Engines: Two 11,905 lb. (5,400 kg.) s.t. Soloviev D-20P turbofans. *Span:*
83 ft. 9½ in. (25·55 m.). *Length:* 100 ft. 4 in. (30·58 m.). *Wing area:* 1,280·9
sq. ft. (119·00 sq. m.). *Maximum take-off weight:* 83,775 lb. (38,000 kg.).
Maximum cruising speed: 540 m.p.h. (870 km/hr.) at 32,800 ft. (10,000 m.).
Range with maximum payload of 13,228 lb. (6,000 kg.): 760 miles (1,220 km.).

51

Boeing 737–293 operated by Air California, *ca* 1969. *Engines:* Two 14,500 lb. (6,575 kg.) s.t. Pratt & Whitney JT8D–9 turbofans. *Span:* 93 ft. 0 in. (28·35 m.). *Length:* 100 ft. 0 in. (30·48 m.). *Wing area:* 980·0 sq. ft. (91·05 sq. m.). *Maximum take-off weight:* 114,500 lb. (51,925 kg.). *Maximum cruising speed:* 568 m.p.h. (915 km/hr.) at 21,900 ft. (6,675 m.). *Range with maximum payload of 35,349 lb. (16,030 kg.):* 2,135 miles (3,435 km.).

52

Dassault Mercure, envisaged in the livery of Air Inter, 1971. *Engines:* Two 15,500 lb. (7,030 kg.) s.t. Pratt & Whitney JT8D–15 turbofans. *Span:* 100 ft. 3 in. (30·55 m.). *Length:* 111 ft. 6 in. (34·00 m.). *Wing area:* 1,248·6 sq. ft. (116·00 sq. m.). *Maximum take-off weight:* 114,640 lb. (52,000 kg.). *Maximum cruising speed:* 587 m.p.h. (945 km/hr.) at 20,000 ft. (6,100 m.). *Maximum range with 134 passengers and reserves:* 1,100 miles (1,772 km.).

CARAVELLE (France)

53

Aérospatiale Caravelle VI—N *Canopo* of Alitalia, *ca* 1965. *Engines:* Two 12,200 lb. (5,535 kg.) s.t. Rolls-Royce Avon Mk. 531 turbojets. *Span:* 112 ft. 6 in. (34·30 m.). *Length:* 105 ft. 0 in. (32·01 m.). *Wing area:* 1,579·1 sq. ft. (146·70 sq. m.). *Maximum take-off weight:* 105,820 lb. (48,000 kg.). *Maximum cruising speed:* 525 m.p.h. (845 km/hr.) at 25,000 ft. (7,620 m.). *Service ceiling:* 32,800 ft. (10,000 m.). *Range with 16,800 lb. (7,620 kg.) payload:* 1,553 miles (2,500 km.).

CARAVELLE (France)

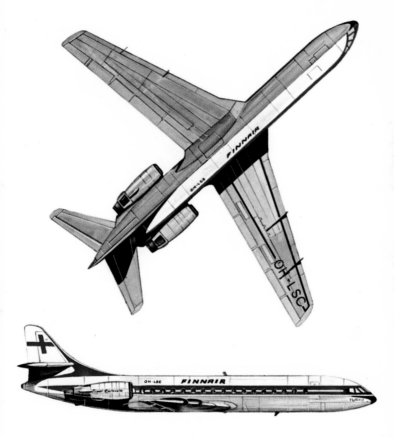

54

Aérospatiale Caravelle Super B *Turku* of Aero O/Y (Finnair), *ca* 1966. *Engines:*
Two 14,000 lb. (6,350 kg.) s.t. Pratt & Whitney JT8D–1 turbofans. *Span:*
112 ft. 6 in. (34·30 m.). *Length:* 108 ft. 3½ in. (33·01 m.). *Wing area:* 1,579·1
sq. ft. (146·70 sq. m.). *Maximum take-off weight:* 114,640 lb. (52,000 kg.).
Maximum cruising speed: 512 m.p.h. (825 km/hr.) at 25,000 ft. (7,620 m.).
Service ceiling: 32,800 ft. (10,000 m.). *Range with maximum payload of
20,060 lb. (9,100 kg.):* 1,650 miles (2,655 km.).

ONE-ELEVEN (U.K.)

55

BAC One-Eleven Model 203 of Braniff International Airways, *ca* 1965. *Engines:* Two 10,330 lb. (4,686 kg.) s.t. Rolls-Royce Spey—25 Mk. 506 turbofans. *Span:* 88 ft. 6 in. (26·97 m.). *Length:* 93 ft. 6 in. (28·50 m.). *Wing area:* 1,003·0 sq. ft. (93·18 sq. m.). *Maximum take-off weight:* 79,000 lb. (35,833 kg.). *Maximum cruising speed:* 541 m.p.h. (871 km/hr.) at 21,000 ft. (6,400 m.). *Maximum cruising height:* 35,000 ft. (10,670 m.). *Range with maximum payload of 17,595 lb. (7,981 kg.):* 875 miles (1,410 km.).

56

BAC One-Eleven Model 518 of Court Line, 1970. *Engines:* Two 12,550 lb. (5,692 kg.) s.t. Rolls-Royce Spey Mk. 512·DW turbofans. *Span:* 93 ft. 6 in. (28·50 m.). *Length:* 107 ft. 0 in. (32·61 m.). *Wing area:* 1,031·0 sq. ft. (95·78 sq. m.). *Maximum take-off weight:* 104,500 lb. (47,400 kg.). *Maximum cruising speed:* 541 m.p.h. (871 km/hr.) at 21,000 ft. (6,400 m.). *Maximum cruising height:* 35,000 ft. (10,670 m.). *Range with typical payload:* 1,692 miles (2,720 km.).

McDONNELL DOUGLAS DC-9 (U.S.A.)

57

McDonnell Douglas DC–9–10 Model 14 of Air Canada, *ca* 1967. *Engines:* Two 14,000 lb. (6,350 kg.) s.t. Pratt & Whitney JT8D–1 turbofans. *Span:* 89 ft. 5 in. (27·25 m.). *Length:* 104 ft. 4¾ in. (31·82 m.). *Wing area:* 934·3 sq. ft. (86·77 sq. m.). *Maximum take-off weight:* 90,700 lb. (41,140 kg.). *Maximum cruising speed:* 561 m.p.h. (903 km/hr.) at 25,000 ft. (7,620 m.). *Range with 50 passengers:* 1,310 miles (2,110 km.).

58

VFW—Fokker VFW 614G1 first prototype in manufacturer's livery, 1971. *Engines:* Two 7,606 lb. (3,450 kg.) s.t. Rolls-Royce/SNECMA M45H—01—15 turbofans. *Span:* 70 ft. 6½ in. (21·50 m.). *Length:* 67 ft. 7 in. (20·60 m.). *Wing area:* 688·9 sq. ft. (64·00 sq. m.). *Maximum take-off weight:* 41,006 lb. (18,600 kg.). *Maximum cruising speed:* 449 m.p.h. (722 km/hr.) at 25,000 ft. (7,620 m.). *Service ceiling:* 24,925 ft. (7,600 m.). *Range with 40 passengers:* 414 miles (667 km.).

FELLOWSHIP (Netherlands)

59

Fokker—VFW F.28 Fellowship Mk. 1000, Colombian Presidential transport, 1971. *Engines:* Two 9,850 lb. (4,468 kg.) s.t. Rolls-Royce Spey Mk. 555—15 turbofans. *Span:* 77 ft. $4\frac{1}{4}$ in. (23·58 m.). *Length:* 89 ft. $10\frac{3}{4}$ in. (27·40 m.). *Wing area:* 822·4 sq. ft. (76·40 sq. m.). *Maximum take-off weight:* 65,000 lb. (29,485 kg.). *Maximum cruising speed:* 528 m.p.h. (849 km/hr.) at 21,000 ft. (6,400 m.). *Range with maximum payload of 14,380 lb. (6,522 kg.):* 1,122 miles (1,805 km.).

60

Tupolev Tu-134 of Polskie Linie Lotnicze (LOT), 1967. *Engines:* Two 14,990 lb. (6,800 kg.) s.t. Soloviev D-30 turbofans. *Span:* 95 ft. 1¾ in. (29·00 m.). *Length:* 114 ft. 10 in. (35·00 m.). *Wing area:* 1,370·3 sq. ft. (127·30 sq. m.). *Maximum take-off weight:* 98,105 lb. (44,500 kg.). *Maximum cruising speed:* 559 m.p.h. (900 km/hr.) at 27,900 ft. (8,500 m.). *Service ceiling:* 39,375 ft. (12,000 m.). *Range with maximum payload of 16,975 lb. (7,700 kg.):* 1,225 miles (1,970 km.).

TRIDENT (U.K.)

61

Hawker Siddeley Trident 3B, first aircraft for British European Airways, 1971. *Engines:* Three 11,960 lb. (5,425 kg.) s.t. Rolls-Royce Spey Mk. 512–5W turbofans and one 5,250 lb. (2,381 kg.) s.t. Rolls-Royce RB.162–86 turbojet. *Span:* 98 ft. 0 in. (29·87 m.). *Length:* 131 ft. 2 in. (39·98 m.). *Wing area:* 1,493·0 sq. ft. (138·70 sq. m.). *Maximum take-off weight:* 150,000 lb. (68,040 kg.). *Maximum cruising speed:* 601 m.p.h. (967 km/hr.) at 28,300 ft. (8,625 m.). *Range with maximum payload of 32,396 lb. (14,695 kg.):* 1,094 miles (1,760 km.).

62

Boeing 727–130 *Kiel* of Deutsche Lufthansa A.G., *ca* 1965. *Engines:* Three 14,000 lb. (6,350 kg.) s.t. Pratt & Whitney JT8D–7 turbofans. *Span:* 108 ft. 0 in. (32·92 m.). *Length:* 133 ft. 2 in. (40·59 m.). *Wing area:* 1,700·0 sq. ft. (157·90 sq. m.). *Typical maximum take-off weight:* 160,000 lb. (72,575 kg.). *Maximum cruising speed:* 605 m.p.h. (974 km/hr.) at 19,000 ft. (5,800 m.). *Service ceiling:* 37,400 ft. (11,400 m.). *Range with maximum payload of 29,000 lb. (13,154 kg.):* 1,900 miles (3,060 km.).

Yak-40 (U.S.S.R.)

63

Yakovlev Yak–40, early production aircraft, operated by Aeroflot *ca* 1968. Data apply to 1971 production version. *Engines:* Three 3,307 lb. (1,500 kg.) s.t. Ivchenko AI–25 turbofans. *Span:* 82 ft. $0\frac{1}{4}$ in. (25·00 m.). *Length:* 66 ft. $9\frac{1}{2}$ in. (20·36 m.). *Wing area:* 753·5 sq. ft. (70·00 sq. m.). *Maximum take-off weight:* 32,408 lb. (14,700 kg.). *Maximum cruising speed:* 342 m.p.h. (550 km/hr.) at 19,685 ft. (6,000 m.). *Range with maximum payload of 5,070 lb. (2,300 kg.):* 590 miles (950 km.).

64

Tupolev Tu-154 prototype in Aeroflot livery, 1971. *Engines:* Three 20,945 lb.
(9,500 kg.) s.t. Kuznetsov NK—8—2 turbofans. *Span:* 123 ft. 2½ in. (37·55 m.).
Length: 157 ft. 1¾ in. (47·90 m.). *Wing area:* 2,168·4 sq. ft. (201·45 sq. m.).
Maximum take-off weight: 198,415 lb. (90,000 kg.). *Maximum cruising speed:*
559 m.p.h. (900 km/hr.) at 36,000 ft. (11,000 m.). *Normal operating altitude:*
36,000 ft. (11,000 m.). *Range with maximum payload of 44,090 lb. (20,000 kg.):*
1,553 miles (2,500 km.).

TRISTAR (U.S.A.)

65

Lockheed L–1011–1 TriStar, third aircraft in Eastern Air Lines livery, 1971. *Engines:* Three 40,600 lb. (18,415 kg.) s.t. Rolls-Royce RB.211–22–02 turbofans. *Span:* 155 ft. 4 in. (47·35 m.). *Length:* 178 ft. 8 in. (54·35 m.). *Wing area:* 3,456·0 sq. ft. (321·07 sq. m.). *Maximum take-off weight:* 409,000 lb. (185,550 kg.). *Maximum cruising speed:* 562 m.p.h. (904 km/hr.) at 35,000 ft. (10,670 m.). *Service ceiling:* 35,000 ft. (10,670 m.). *Range with maximum payload of 87,811 lb. (39,830 kg.):* 3,285 miles (5,290 km.).

McDONNELL DOUGLAS DC-10 (U.S.A.)

66

McDonnell Douglas DC-10 Series 10, second aircraft in American Airlines livery, 1971. *Engines:* Three 40,000 lb. (18,144 kg.) s.t. General Electric CF6–6 turbofans. *Span:* 155 ft. 4 in. (47·35 m.). *Length:* 181 ft. 5 in. (55·29 m.). *Wing area:* 3,861·0 sq. ft. (358·70 sq. m.). *Maximum take-off weight:* 430,000 lb. (195,040 kg.). *Maximum cruising speed:* 587 m.p.h. (945 km/hr.) at 31,000 ft. (9,450 m.). *Service ceiling:* 35,000 ft. (10,670 m.). *Range with 78,000 lb. (35,380 kg.) payload:* 2,760 miles (4,440 km.).

COMET 4 (U.K.)

67

Hawker Siddeley Comet 4C of United Arab Airlines, *ca* 1964. *Engines:* Four 10,500 lb. (4,763 kg.) s.t. Rolls-Royce Avon Mk. 525B turbojets. *Span:* 114 ft. 10 in. (35·00 m.). *Length:* 118 ft. 0 in. (35·97 m.). *Wing area:* 2,121·0 sq. ft. (197·05 sq. m.). *Maximum take-off weight:* 162,000 lb. (73,500 kg.). *Typical cruising speed:* 542 m.p.h. (872 km/hr.) at 31,000 ft. (9,450 m.). *Service ceiling:* 39,000 ft. (11,890 m.). *Range with 19,630 lb. (8,900 kg.) payload:* 2,590 miles (4,168 km.).

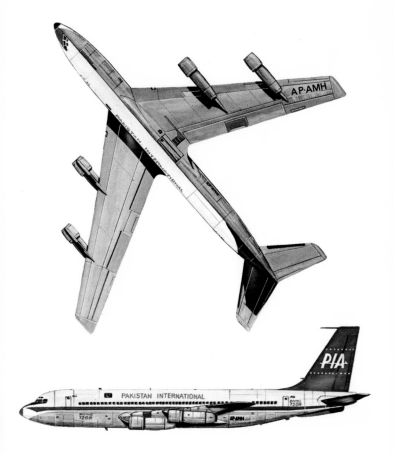

68

Boeing 720–040B of Pakistan International Airlines Corporation, *ca* 1963.
Engines: Four 17,000 lb. (7,710 kg.) s.t. Pratt & Whitney JT3D–1 turbofans.
Span: 130 ft. 10 in. (39·87 m.). *Length:* 136 ft. 9 in. (41·68 m.). *Wing area:*
2,521·0 sq. ft. (234·21 sq. m.). *Maximum take-off weight:* 234,000 lb.
(106,140 kg.). *Maximum cruising speed:* 611 m.p.h. (983 km/hr.) at 25,000
ft. (7,620 m.). *Service ceiling:* 42,000 ft. (12,800 m.). *Range with maximum
payload of 43,117 lb. (19,692 kg.):* 4,155 miles (6,690 km.).

McDONNELL DOUGLAS DC-8 (U.S.A.)

69

McDonnell Douglas DC–8–51 of Aeronaves de Mexico S.A., *ca* 1965. *Engines:*
Four 18,000 lb. (8,172 kg.) s.t. Pratt & Whitney JT3D–3 turbofans. *Span:*
142 ft. 5 in. (43·41 m.). *Length:* 150 ft. 6 in. (45·87 m.). *Wing area:* 2,773·0
sq. ft. (257·62 sq. m.). *Maximum take-off weight:* 315,000 lb. (142,880 kg.).
Maximum cruising speed: 579 m.p.h. (932 km/hr.) at 30,000 ft. (9,150 m.).
Range with maximum payload of 34,360 lb. (15,585 kg.): 5,720 miles
(9,205 km.).

CONVAIR 880 (U.S.A.)

70

Convair 880–M of Civil Air Transport (Taiwan), *ca* 1962. *Engines:* Four 11,650 lb. (5,285 kg.) s.t. General Electric CJ805–3B turbojets. *Span:* 120 ft. 0 in. (36·58 m.). *Length:* 129 ft. 4 in. (39·42 m.). *Wing area:* 2,000·0 sq. ft. (185·81 sq. m.). *Maximum take-off weight:* 193,000 lb. (87,540 kg.). *Maximum cruising speed:* 615 m.p.h. (990 km/hr.) at 22,500 ft. (6,860 m.). *Service ceiling:* 41,000 ft. (12,500 m.). *Range with 24,000 lb. (10,885 kg.) payload:* 2,880 miles (4,630 km.).

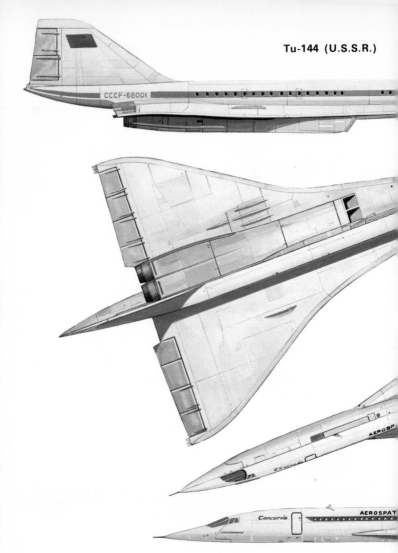

Tu-144 (U.S.S.R.)

CCCP-68001

71

Tupolev Tu–144 first prototype in the colours of Aeroflot, *ca* 1970. *Engines:*
Four 28,660/38,580 lb. (13,000/17,500 kg.) s.t. Kuznetsov NK–144 afterburning turbofans. *Span:* 88 ft. 7 in. (27·00 m.). *Length:* 190 ft. 3½ in. (58·00 m.).
Maximum take-off weight: 330,000 lb. (150,000 kg.). *Maximum cruising speed:*
1,550 m.p.h. (2,500 km/hr.) at 65,000 ft. (20,000 m.) (Mach 2·35). *Range:*
4,040 miles (6,500 km.).

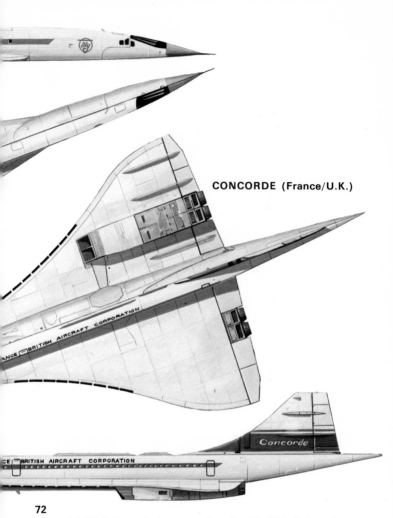

CONCORDE (France/U.K.)

72

Aérospatiale/BAC Concorde (pre-production aircraft), 1971. Data apply to initial production version. *Engines:* Four 38,050 lb. (17,260 kg.) s.t. Rolls-Royce Bristol/SNECMA Olympus 593B series turbojets. *Span:* 84 ft. 0 in. (25·60 m.). *Length:* 203 ft. 11½ in. (62·17 m.). *Wing area:* 3,856·0 sq. ft. (358·25 sq. m.). *Maximum take-off weight:* 385,000 lb. (174,640 kg.). *Maximum cruising speed:* 1,450 m.p.h. (2,333 km/hr.) at 54,500 ft. (16,600 m.) (Mach 2·2). *Range at Mach 2·2 with typical payload of 28,000 lb. (12,700 kg.):* 4,020 miles (6,470 km.).

BOEING 707 INTERCONTINENTAL (U.S.A.)

73

Boeing 707–437 *Kanchenjunga* of Air-India, *ca* 1962. *Engines:* Four 17,500 lb. (7,945 kg.) s.t. Rolls-Royce Conway Mk. 508 turbofans. *Span:* 142 ft. 5 in. (43·41 m.). *Length:* 152 ft. 11 in. (46·61 m.). *Wing area:* 2,892·0 sq. ft. (268·68 sq. m.). *Maximum take-off weight:* 312,000 lb. (141,520 kg.). *Maximum cruising speed:* 593 m.p.h. (954 km/hr.) at 25,000 ft. (7,620 m.). *Service ceiling:* 42,000 ft. (12,800 m.). *Range with maximum payload of 57,000 lb. (25,855 kg.):* 4,865 miles (7,830 km.).

CONVAIR 990A (U.S.A.)

74

Convair 990A Coronado *Vaud* of Schweizerische Luftverkehr A.G. (Swissair), *ca* 1966. *Engines:* Four 16,050 lb. (7,280 kg.) s.t. General Electric CJ805—23B turbofans. *Span:* 120 ft. 0 in. (36·58 m.). *Length:* 139 ft. 2½ in. (42·43 m.). *Wing area:* 2,250·0 sq. ft. (209·03 sq. m.). *Maximum take-off weight:* 253,000 lb. (114,760 kg.). *Maximum cruising speed:* 625 m.p.h. (1,006 km/hr.) at 21,000 ft. (6,400 m.). *Service ceiling:* 41,000 ft. (12,500 m.). *Range with 25,770 lb. (11,690 kg.) payload:* 3,800 miles (6,115 km.).

SUPER VC10 (U.K.)

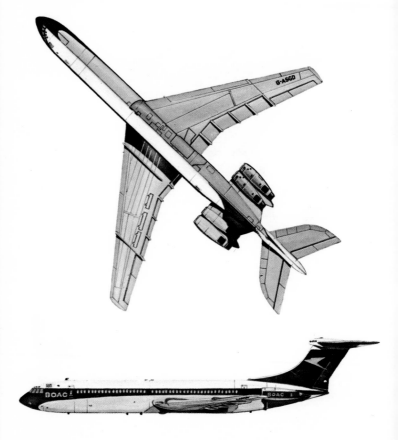

75

BAC Super VC10 Model 1151 of British Overseas Airways Corporation, *ca* 1965.
Engines: Four 22,500 lb. (10,205 kg.) s.t. Rolls-Royce Conway 43 Mk. 550
turbofans. *Span:* 146 ft. 2 in. (44·55 m.). *Length:* 171 ft. 8 in. (52·32 m.). *Wing
area:* 2,887·0 sq. ft. (268·21 sq. m.). *Maximum take-off weight:* 335,000 lb.
(151,950 kg.). *Maximum cruising speed:* 568 m.p.h. (914 km/hr.) at 38,000 ft.
(11,600 m.). *Service ceiling:* 42,000 ft. (12,800 m.). *Range with maximum
payload of 50,406 lb. (22,860 kg.):* 4,630 miles (7,450 km.).

Il-62 (U.S.S.R.)

76

Ilyushin Il–62 of CSA, *ca* 1967. *Engines:* Four 23,150 lb. (10,500 kg.) s.t.
Kuznetsov NK–8–4 turbofans. *Span:* 141 ft. 9 in. (43·20 m.). *Length:* 174 ft.
3½ in. (53·12 m.). *Wing area:* 3,009·05 sq. ft. (279·55 sq. m.). *Maximum take-off
weight:* 352,740 lb. (160,000 kg.). *Maximum cruising speed:* 560 m.p.h.
(900 km/hr.) at 42,600 ft. (13,000 m.). *Range with maximum payload of
50,700 lb. (23,000 kg.):* 4,350 miles (7,000 km.).

77

Boeing 747–143 *Neil Armstrong* of Alitalia, 1970. *Engines:* Four 43,500 lb. (19,730 kg.) s.t. Pratt & Whitney JT9D–3 turbofans. *Span:* 195 ft. 8 in. (59·64 m.). *Length:* 231 ft. 4 in. (70·51 m.). *Wing area:* 5,500·0 sq. ft. (510·97 sq. m.). *Maximum take-off weight:* 710,000 lb. (322,050 kg.). *Maximum level speed:* 595 m.p.h. (958 km/hr.) at 30,000 ft. (9,150 m.). *Maximum cruising height:* 45,000 ft. (13,715 m.). *Range with maximum payload of 177,684 lb. (80,596 kg.):* 5,790 miles (9,140 km.).

I-DEMA

McDONNELL DOUGLAS DC-8 SUPER SIXTY (U.S.A.)

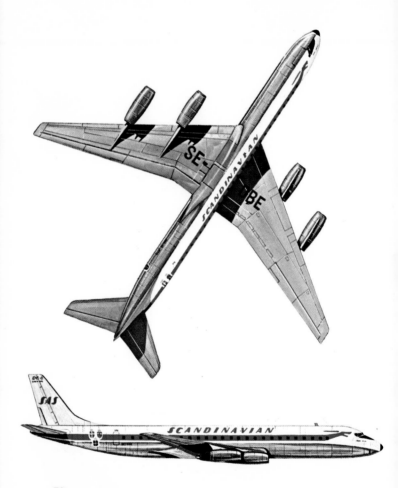

78

McDonnell Douglas DC–8–62 *Anund Viking* of Scandinavian Airlines System, *ca* 1967. *Engines:* Four 18,000 lb. (8,172 kg.) s.t. Pratt & Whitney JT3D–3B turbofans. *Span:* 148 ft. 5 in. (45·23 m.). *Length:* 157 ft. 5 in. (47·98 m.). *Wing area:* 2,927·0 sq. ft. (271·93 sq. m.). *Maximum take-off weight:* 335,000 lb. (151,950 kg.). *Maximum cruising speed:* 600 m.p.h. (965 km/hr.) at 30,000 ft. (9,150 m.). *Range with maximum payload of 47,335 lb. (21,470 kg.):* 6,000 miles (9,640 km.).

1 Curtiss C-46

Arising out of talks held in 1936 between the Curtiss-Wright Corporation and a number of US domestic airlines, the CW-20 (as the design was originally known) materialised three years later as the world's largest twin-engined transport and featured a generous 'double-bubble' fuselage. The twin-tailed CW-20 prototype, NX19436, powered by two 1,700 hp Wright R-586-C14-BA2 Double Row Cyclones, flew for the first time on 26 March 1940. After substitution of the now familiar single fin and rudder, the aircraft was evaluated briefly by the USAAF (as the C-55-CS), and then sold to BOAC in 1941 as G-AGDI *St Louis*, being used as a 24-seat war transport for the next two years. Commercial production of the CW-20 was precluded by America's entry into World War 2, but under the name Commando an unpressurised, Double Wasp-powered version was accepted for a military role. A description of the C-46/R5C-1 Commando appears in the *Bombers 1939–45* volume. Plans were made after the war to produce a CW-20E civil version for Eastern; but this failed to achieve production status. Instead, several hundred war-surplus Commandos were 'de-militarised' for the commercial market. Their adoption by civil operators was slow to reach appreciable proportions, largely due to some difficulty in meeting full CAA requirements regarding maximum operating weights. However, by 1960 over ninety carriers were oper-ating C-46's, and there were still about two hundred of these aircraft in airline service at the beginning of 1970, mostly in North and South America. The majority of those which have served post-war are former C-46A's (single loading door), C-46D's (double cargo doors and modified nose), or generally similar C-46F's; these have R-2800-51M1 engines, a 17,600 lb (7,983 kg) payload and 48,000 lb (21,772 kg) gross weight. Post-war modifications have included the 1956 CW-20T with various structural improvements, introduced by Air Carrier Engineering Services and the L.B. Smith Aircraft Corporation; the Super 46C, from the same source in 1958 with a 50,650 lb (22,975 kg) gross weight; and a similar version introduced by Riddle Airlines in 1957 as the C-46R.

2 Ilyushin Il-14 ('Crate')

For many years the piston-engined workhorse of the air forces and air-lines in the Soviet Union and numerous satellite states, the Il-14 is still in commercial service, though in diminishing numbers: excluding those still operated by Aeroflot, more than a hundred were esti-mated to be still active early in 1970. The Il-14 is a derivative of Ilyushin's earlier Il-12, the design of which was begun in 1943 as a potential successor to the Li-2 (licence DC-3) built extensively in Russia during the war years. Construction of the prototype Il-12 (CCCP-L1380) began in 1945, and the aeroplane made its first flight early in 1946, its existence being made public in August of that year. The first transport to be built post-war in the Soviet Union, it was in production from 1946–53, during which time over three thousand are believed to have been built, most of them for military use. The original production Il-12, with 1,650 hp ASh-82FN engines, was supplanted by the Il-12B, which had a number of refinements including a small dorsal fin fairing and a strengthened nosewheel oleo. Both versions had unpressurised fuselages, accommodating a flight crew of four and 27 passengers; they served with Aeroflot and Il-12B's were operated by the Czechoslovak and Polish state airlines, CSA and LOT. In 1953 the Il-12 was superseded in production by the Il-14, a development of the former and distinguishable by its more powerful engines, revised wings with squared-off tips, and a larger and more angular vertical tail. In its original standard commercial version, the Il-14P, the new type seated only 18 passengers, although between 1956–59 about eighty examples of a 26-seat version were built under licence by the VEB Flugzeugbau of Dresden. The first VEB-built Il-14P was flown in April 1956, and aircraft from the Dresden production batch were supplied to airlines in Bulgaria, China, Hungary and Poland, as well as to the former East German Lufthansa. Licence production of the Il-14P was also undertaken by Avia in Czechoslovakia, who built fifty for the USSR, six for the national airline, CSA, and one for LOT. By far the most prolific model,

however, has been the Il-14M, which first appeared in 1956 and entered service with Aeroflot in the summer of that year. Chief differences noticeable in the Il-14M are a 3 ft 3¼ in (1·00 m) longer fuselage, with seats for 24–32 passengers, and a slightly different wing planform. The Il-14M was subsequently built in many thousands in Russia (up to 1958), Czechoslovakia and East Germany for use both as a civil and a military transport. The Avia company refined the aircraft still further during its production period, which ended in 1962. The original Il-14M was produced as the Avia 14-32A in 1957, Avia 14T cargo transport, and finally by the Avia 14 Super, later known as the 14 Salon. Considerable structural redesign of this last-named version has resulted in a much lower basic empty weight, a somewhat higher gross weight and additional range through the use of wingtip fuel tanks. Passenger cabin windows are circular in the 14 Salon, which can seat up to 42 passengers and has a pressurised fuselage.

3 Douglas DC-3

One of the most challenging activities for a high proportion of the world's aircraft designers and airline chiefs in recent years has been the pursuit of an elusive and almost non-existent will-o'-the-wisp described as the 'DC-3 replacement'; for how does one begin to set about replacing a thirty-five-year-old aeroplane that in 1970 was still in the inventory of more than two hundred airlines, large and small, in every part of the globe, performing every kind of task imaginable? For a large percentage of the years since the end of World War 2, the DC-3's in commercial service outnumbered the total of all other types of transport aeroplane put together. A detailed *Flight International* survey published in December 1969 revealed nearly nine hundred DC-3's still in airline service. The evolution of the DC-3, as a 'sleeper' development of the DC-2, began in 1935, with the first flight taking place later that year on 17 December. In the event, however, it was the day transport version which attracted most customer attention and became the principal production model prior to the outbreak of World War 2. The war brought about a tremendous output of these aircraft – nearly eleven thousand in the United States, together with some two thousand built under licence in the Soviet Union (as the Lisunov Li-2) and another four hundred and fifty in Japan as the L2D2. When the war ended, thousands of surplus C-47's and other military variants flooded the civil market and were snapped up eagerly by operators the world over for passenger, freight and general duties. A year or two later the DC-3 went through a rather bad patch, acquiring a reputation for being accident-prone – though the very number of them in service, by the law of averages, must have precluded an entirely trouble-free career. Some of these accidents were undoubtedly due to overloading: nominally, the DC-3's capacity is 28–32 passengers, but there were

plenty of hair-raising tales of more than twice this number being herded into some aircraft in Middle Eastern and African countries – perhaps due to the faith of simple people in the DC-3's ability to do almost anything asked of it – though most of these trips were accomplished without incident. Time, and the DC-3's sterling contribution to the Berlin airlift, erased the 'death-trap' image from the public mind, and it has enjoyed a virtually unblemished career ever since. Because of the widespread nature of the DC-3's employment, it would be impossible to list here the innumerable modifications, official and unofficial, that have been carried out during its past twenty-five years of service. Generally speaking, these concern the employment of varying types of engine, including turboprops, differing shapes of passenger cabin windows and the arrangement of internal seating and furnishing. Most of those still in service are DC-3C's, a structurally strengthened version of the wartime C-47 Skytrain or Dakota. In addition, several thousand military models continue in service with the air arms of over seventy countries, including those of the United States.

4 **Vickers Viking**
The longevity of the Viking is typified by the machine chosen for the illustration on page 20: as the first production example of the long-nosed Viking 1B, it made its maiden flight on 6 August 1946, yet was disposed of for scrap by its original owner only in 1962. As

Britain's first post-war civil transport to enter commercial service, the Viking was the result of a requirement issued in 1944 for a 'Wellington transport', and the three prototypes and first production model (the Viking 1A) utilised the geodetic-pattern outer wing panels, engine nacelles and landing gear assemblies of the celebrated wartime bomber. With two 1,675 hp Hercules 130 engines, the first prototype (G-AGOK) was flown at Wisley on 22 June 1945; G-AGOL and 'OM joined it before the end of the year, both of these featuring a curved dorsal fin extension which became standard on production aircraft. The Viking's C of A was issued on 24 April 1946. Nineteen Viking 1A's, with 1,690 hp Hercules 630's, were built, eleven of them going to BEA. On 1 September 1946 the first Viking services (Northolt–Copenhagen) were inaugurated by BEA. Production continued with thirty-one Viking 1's, with more conventional stressed-skin exteriors replacing the fabric-covered geodetic components, and these also were delivered chiefly to BEA and various associate airlines. Five 1A's were brought up to Viking 1 standard and operated by British West Indian Airways. The major version was the Viking 1B, one hundred and thirteen of which were built before production ceased at the end of 1947. Like the Viking 1, the 1B was powered by 1,690 hp Hercules 634 radials, but differed in having a 2 ft 4 in (0·71 m) longer fuselage with seating capacity increased from 21 to 24 initially, and eventually to 27. Viking 1B's were sold or leased to carriers in Africa, Argentina, Denmark, Eire, India, Iraq, Southern Rhodesia and the United Kingdom, operating both on scheduled services and with a large number of charter operators. As late as 1960 there were still about a hundred Vikings in service, but by 1970 the number had dwindled to three, belonging to the French operator Europe Aero Service. Various internal modifications enabled some Vikings to carry heavier loads than those originally specified, for example the 'Mks 3/3A/3B' (unofficial designation of 1/1A/1B's operated by Eagle), with an additional half-ton of payload, and BEA's 'Admiral' class of 1952, which seated a maximum of 36 passengers. Variants of the design included the RAF Viking C.2, Valetta and Varsity, small numbers of which appeared on the civil register in the 1950s. One distinction belonging to the Viking is that of G-AJPH, the Nene engine testbed, which on 6 April 1948 became the first purely jet-powered British transport aeroplane to fly.

5 Saab 90 Scandia

In broadly the same class as the Convair 240, Il-12 and Viking, the Scandia's design was begun by Saab in 1944 under the title Project CT. Later the designation Saab 90 was allocated, and the prototype (SE-BCA) was flown for the first time on 16 November 1946. This machine, powered by two 1,350 hp Pratt & Whitney R-2000-2SD13-G engines, was widely demonstrated in the major European countries during 1947–48, but failed to collect more than one order, and that (for ten aircraft) from the home airline AB Aerotransport, which became a part of the SAS combine in February 1948. Six of the ABA order were delivered to SAS, the remaining four going to Aerovias Brasil. Two years later, Aerovias became part of VASP, which ordered a further five Scandias, and these were the only airlines to operate the type. In all, seventeen production Scandias were built, the last two being for SAS. The first eleven aircraft were completed entirely by Saab. The remaining six, because of Saab's heavy commitments to military production, were undertaken with assistance from the Aviolanda, de Schelde and Fokker factories in Holland. The production model, with more powerful engines of the R-2180 type, was known as the Saab 90A-2, and was introduced on SAS's Scandinavian domestic services in November 1950. It carried a flight crew of four (later reduced to three) and provided accommodation for 24–32 passengers in a non-pressurised fuselage. Seating capacity was later increased to 36. After their withdrawal from SAS service in 1957 the domestic Scandias were also bought by VASP, and with the purchase of the prototype by the same airline, all aircraft of this type gravitated to Brazil. In South America they have continued a lengthy flying career. In 1967 there were still nine Scandias in the VASP fleet. Two other variants of the Scandia were projected: the

Saab 90A-3, enlarged to seat up to 38 passengers, and the Saab 90B-3, with similar capacity and a pressurised fuselage; but neither of these was built.

6 Airspeed Ambassador
The A.S.57 Ambassador resulted from the Brabazon Committee's requirement IIA for a European short-haul airliner (Specification 25/43), and work on building a prototype was started in 1945. Originally the aeroplane was scheduled to have Centaurus 130 engines and a capacity ranging from 28–50 seats, depending on stage length, though in BEA service the normal range was 40–47 seats. The first prototype (G-AGUA), powered by two 2,600 hp Centaurus 631 radials, flew at Christchurch on 10 July 1947, and from the outset it was evident that the design had great passenger appeal. The high wing permitted an extremely quiet and roomy passenger cabin, which offered an excellent view from the large panoramic windows. Cleanliness and elegance of line were apparent throughout the aeroplane, down to the interchangeable 'power eggs', each in a petal-type cowling specially designed by Airspeed to offer minimum drag. Furthermore, the Ambassador combined modest runway requirements with an outstanding single-engined performance. The second prototype (G-AKRD) flew on 26 August 1948; two static-test airframes were built, followed by one pre-production Ambassador (G-ALFR) which was used to obtain the C of A and for

route proving by BEA. This aircraft had the definitive Centaurus 661 powerplant, and flew for the first time in May 1950. Twenty production Ambassadors were built for BEA, the first of these flying on 12 January 1951. Airline acceptance trials were completed during the following August, and on 13 March 1952, under the BEA class name 'Elizabethan', the Ambassador entered service. It quickly proved to have better operating costs, especially over the shorter routes, than any other aircraft in the BEA fleet, and remained in service with the airline for five and a half years until the latter half of 1957. Three were then operated for a short time by Butler Air Transport, two others by Globe Air, and another pair by the Royal Jordanian Air Force. These all returned eventually to the United Kingdom, where for several more years they flew with BKS, Dan-Air and other operators. One was still operating with Dan-Air in 1971. In the latter 1950s, G-AKRD and G-ALZR were extensively used as flying testbeds for Dart, Eland, Proteus and Tyne engines, and various turboprop developments (including one with four Darts) were projected under the designation A.S.59. Other projects included the A.S.60 Ayrshire, a military transport to Specification 13/45, and the A.S.67 freighter, but none of these came to fruition.

7 Martin 2-0-2 and 4-0-4

The Martin 2-0-2 made its first appearance slightly ahead of the Convair 240, and on 13 August 1947 became the first twin-engined airliner of US post-war design to receive a CAA type operating certificate. Two flying prototypes were built, the maiden flight taking place on 22 November 1946, and a third airframe was completed for static testing. Twenty-five 2-0-2's were produced to the order of Northwest Orient Airlines, plus four for LAN-Chile and two for LAV of Venezuela, LAN-Chile being first to put the type into service in October 1947. Powered by two 2,400 hp R-2800-CA18 engines, the Martin 2-0-2 seated 36–40 passengers in an unpressurised fuselage. In 1948, investigation of an accident to an airline 2-0-2 revealed some structural weaknesses in the wing; all aircraft then in service were temporarily withdrawn for this to be rectified, and no further 2-0-2's were built. Two pressurised developments were proposed, the passenger 3-0-3 and the cargo 3-0-4, and a prototype of the former was flown on 20 June 1947, but in 1949 both designs were shelved in favour of the Martin 4-0-4. Initial orders for the 4-0-4 were placed by Eastern and TWA, for thirty-five and thirty respectively, and as an interim measure twelve Martin 2-0-2A's (the first of which flew in July 1950) were built for use by the latter airline. These were unpressurised, but had -CB16 engines of 2,400 hp and a gross weight of 43,000 lb (19,504 kg); they entered TWA service on 1 September 1950. The Martin 4-0-4 had the same powerplant and the same seating capacity as the 2-0-2A, but its pressurised fuselage was 3 ft 3 in (0·99 m) longer and the maximum payload and take-off weight were increased to 11,592 lb (5,259 kg) and 44,900 lb (20,366 kg) respectively. A converted 2-0-2 airframe, N40400, acted as the 4-0-4 prototype, flying for the first time at Baltimore on 21 October 1950. Between autumn 1951 and spring 1953 a total of one hundred and three Martin 4-0-4's were delivered: Eastern and TWA had increased their original orders to sixty and forty-one, and the remaining two aircraft were completed as RM-1's for the US Coast Guard. The Martin 4-0-4 entered service with TWA in October 1951, and with Eastern in January 1952. By the beginning of 1971 about forty Martins were still in airline service. Almost all of these were 4-0-4's, the largest fleets being those of Piedmont Airlines and Southern Airways.

8 & 9 Convair 240/340/440/540/580/600/640 series

A requirement existed in many countries after World War 2 for a twin-engined, medium-range, medium-capacity passenger transport aircraft. Russia produced the Il-12, Britain the Viking, the United States the Martin 2-0-2 and Convairliner; and of these the Convair proved to be the most adaptable and durable. Convair's first medium twin design was the Model 110, a prototype of which (NX90653) was flown for the first time on 8 July 1946. Powered by two 2,100 hp R-2800-S1C3-G engines, the Convair 110

was a 30-seater having a wing span of 89 ft 0 in (27·13 m) and a length of 71 ft 0 in (21·64 m). Though an attractive aeroplane, the 110 offered only limited payload/range capabilities and did not go into production. From it, however, Convair developed the slightly larger Model 240 with 2,400 hp R-2800-CA18 engines. Despite a slimmer-section fuselage the Convair 240 seated up to 40 passengers, and had appreciably better range than its predecessor. The prototype (N24501) was first flown at San Diego on 16 March 1947, and immediately met with favourable reaction. Series production started late in 1947, and by mid-1948 over a hundred and fifty 240's had been ordered. The largest initial order, for seventy-five aircraft, was from American Airlines; other US domestic carriers to order Convairs included Continental (five), Pan American (twenty) and Western (ten). Overseas customers included the Argentine operator FAMA, which ordered five, and KLM, Swissair and TAA, which ordered twelve, four and five respectively. The first certificated Convair 240 was delivered on 28 February 1948 to American, which put the type into scheduled service on 1 June. The first overseas delivery was made to TAA on 25 August the same year. The Model 240 remained in production until 1958, by which time five hundred and seventy-one examples had been built. The majority of these were completed as T-29 aircrew trainers and C-131A transports for the US services, but one hundred and seventy-six were civil 240's. These have served with nearly fifty airlines the world over; about one-sixth of them were still in airline service in 1970, and a number continue to fly as business executive transports.

The basic soundness of the Convair 240 design led, inevitably, to consideration of a stretched version, and this duly appeared in the form of the Convair 340, the prototype of which (N3401) flew for the first time on 5 October 1951. More efficient R-2800-CB16 engines offered a somewhat better performance than that of the Model 240, but the major outward changes in the Model 340 were an increase of 13 ft 7 in (4·14 m) in the wing span and the insertion of additional fuselage sections of 1 ft 4 in (0·40 m) ahead of the wing and 3 ft 2 in (0·96 m) aft. These alterations enabled the Convair 340 to seat up to 44 passengers in a standard interior layout, and by the time the 340 received its FAA type certificate on 28 March 1952 more than a hundred and sixty had been ordered by nearly a score of domestic and overseas operators. The first delivery of a production 340 was made to United Air Lines on 28 March 1952. Two hundred and nine civil 340's were built, of which about two dozen were still in airline operation at the beginning of 1970. Others are in service as company transports.

The Convair 440 Metropolitan retains the same overall configuration as the 340, but has more powerful R-2800-CB17 engines and a number of detail refinements. These include better cabin sound-proofing and, on many aircraft, weather-warning radar. Maximum take-off weight and maximum payload of the Metropolitan are respectively 49,100 lb (22,270 kg) and 12,700 lb (5,760 kg), and the maximum seating capacity is raised to 52. The first Metropolitan, a converted 340, was flown on 6 October 1955, but in addition to 340 conversions one hundred and eighty-six civil 440's were built from the outset to Metropolitan standard, and about a hundred of these were still in service in 1970; the major operators at that time were Eastern in the United States, and Iberia, SAS and Linjeflyg in Europe. Convair-liners of one kind or another have thus been continuously in service for more than twenty years, some of them still with their original 1948 customers.

Conversion of Convair 240 and 340/440 airliners to turbine power has been taking place for more than a decade, though it was only in the early and middle 1960s that the movement gained impetus. There are three basic series of turboprop Convairs, designated according to powerplant. These are the 540, with Napier Eland engines; the 580, with Allisons; and the 600 and 640, with Rolls-Royce Darts. The US Air Force tested a military YC-131C with Allison T56 turboprops in 1954, but it was Napier which started the civil conversion movement when, at the end of that year, it fitted 3,060 ehp Eland N. El. 1 engines to an ex-airline Convair 340. Re-registered G-ANVP, it flew for the first time with Elands on 9 February 1955.

(Some years later, with the uprated Eland 504A's which became the standard installation, this machine was leased to Allegheny Airlines, in whose colours it appears in the drawing on page 25.) Allegheny subsequently operated five more Convair 540's until 1962, when cessation of Eland development led to their withdrawal. One other was converted by the PacAero division of Pacific Airmotive for Butler Air Transport. Canadair undertook to produce Eland Convairs under the title Canadair 540, and converted three 440's, one as a demonstrator and the other two for Quebecair. No further civil orders materialised, but Canadair built ten, as complete aircraft, for the RCAF as CC-109 Cosmopolitans; preceded by the two former Quebecair machines as military prototypes, they were delivered from July 1960. PacAero followed up its original interest in the 540 by proposing the more powerful Convair 580, using 3,750 shp Allison 501D-13 turboprops. With increased tail control surface area, the Convair 580 was certificated in April 1960, although the first to enter service (with Frontier Airlines) did not do so until June 1964. Seating was increased from 44 to 52. The most recent alliance has been that with the 3,025 eshp Rolls-Royce Dart RDa. 10/1 to produce the Convair 600. This conversion, unlike the others, is applied to the Convair 240 as well as the 340/440, although in the former case additional strengthening of the structure is necessary. The first 600 conversion was in fact carried out on a former

Model 240D which, as N94294, made its first flight with Darts on 20 May 1965. The first Convair 600 to enter service was Central Airlines' N74858 on 30 November 1965; Martin's Air Charter became the first European operator of the type in April 1966. With Dart engines, seating can be increased to 48 in former 240's and to 56 in ex-340/440's, the latter being designated Model 640 in their converted form. Caribair, on 22 December 1965, became the first Convair 640 operator.

10   NAMC YS-11

In May 1957 the Japanese Ministry of International Trade and Industry set up a Transport Aircraft Development Association consisting of six of the major aircraft constructors in the country. Its objective was the design and production of an indigenous medium-range commercial transport. After establishing a basic specification for the aeroplane, the TADA set up a committee under Dr Hidemara Kimura to study various design proposals, and by January 1959 a basic configuration had been agreed upon. Work started shortly afterwards on a full-size mock-up of the design. This was carried out at Sugita, Yokohama, and the aeroplane was allotted the designation YS-11. On 1 June 1959 the Nihon Aeroplane Manufacturing Company (NAMC) was created to assume responsibility for development, flight testing and marketing of the aircraft. At this time the YS-11 was cast as a 60/70-seater, but a revision of customer requirements during the next two or three years caused this to be scaled down to 52–60 seats. The first of the two flying prototypes (two others were built for static testing) made its maiden flight on 30 August 1962 and the second on 28 December 1962. The YS-11 entered production in 1964, the first series-built aircraft flying on 23 October of that year. Construction was allocated as follows: tail units to Fuji, main wings and engine nacelles to Kawasaki, main fuselage (and final assembly) to Mitsubishi, flaps and ailerons to Nippi, rear fuselage to Shin Meiwa and honeycomb structural components to Showa. The NAMC was responsible for design work, production and quality control and sales. A domestic C of A was issued for the YS-11 on 25 August 1964, and an FAA certificate for exported models on 18 October 1965. The first YS-11 delivery was made, in March 1965, to Toa Airways, domestic services commencing on 1 April, and before the end of the year the first foreign delivery, to Filipinas Orient Airways, had also been made. The YS-11, the first airliner in service to use the RDa. 10 version of the Dart turboprop, has since acquired a highly satisfactory reputation among its operators, and by the spring of 1971 deliveries had passed the 160 mark. Of the 60-passenger initial production version, designated YS-11-100, forty-seven examples were built, including four for the JASDF and two cargo models for the JMSDF. Subsequent production aircraft have YS-11A designations, beginning with the YS-11A-

200 (60-seat all-passenger version); the YS-11A-300 is a mixed-traffic version, seating 46 passengers and featuring a cargo-loading door at the front; and the YS-11A-400 is an all-cargo counterpart. These have recently been joined by -500, -600 and -700 versions, which correspond broadly to the -200, -300 and -400 but have a 1,102 lb (500 kg) increase in maximum take-off weight. Production was due to end after completion of the 182nd aircraft.

11 Hawker Siddeley 748

The Hawker Siddeley 748 was a somewhat slow starter in the world airliner stakes, but a sales total of two hundred and fifty (including military purchases) was reached in June 1971, of which one hundred and ninety-eight were for export. Design development, as the 20-seat Avro 748, began as early as 1957, but until an enlarged, Dart-powered development of the aeroplane was proposed, the project attracted very little interest from the airlines. Nevertheless, on 9 January 1959, Hawker Siddeley announced its intention to go ahead with the project and build an initial batch of twelve aircraft, and work started a month later on the construction of two flying prototypes and two other aircraft for static tests. Encouragement came in July 1959 when the Indian government announced its intention to assemble the HS 748 under licence at Kanpur as a military transport for the Indian Air Force. The first HS 748 prototype, G-APZV, was flown at Woodford on 24 June 1960, the second

(G-ARAY) on 10 April 1961 and the first production 748 (G-ARMV, one of three for Skyways) on 30 August 1961. This initial production model, known as the Series 1, had a slightly greater wing span than the prototypes, and was powered by 1,880 ehp Dart Mk 514 (RDa. 6) engines. During 1961, components for five Series 1's were despatched to Kanpur for assembly, and the first Indian-assembled machine was flown on 1 November. The HS 748 Series 1 entered airline service with Skyways Coach Air and with Aerolineas Argentinas in April 1962, following the issue of a C of A on 9 January. Meanwhile, on 6 November 1961, G-ARAY had flown for the first time with a new powerplant of 2,105 ehp Dart Mk 531's (RDa. 7's) to act as the prototype for the HS 748 Series 2. This second model, apart from an enhanced performance and higher operating weight, is otherwise similar to the Series 1, which it supplanted in production; both versions have a seating range of 40–58 passengers. The first Series 2 production machine flew in August 1962, and certification of this version followed two months later. The Series 2 is the subject of Indian licence assembly: the first Kanpur HS 748 Srs 2 was flown on 28 January 1964, and orders up to mid-1971 totalled twenty-four for Indian Airlines Corporation and forty for the Indian Air Force. Military orders for British-built 748's have been placed by the Brazilian Air Force (six), Ecuadorean Air Force (one), Royal Australian Air Force and Navy (ten and two), Venezuelan Ministry of Defence (one) and Zambian Air Force (one). Air Support Command operates four under the designation Andover CC. Mk 2, and two others serve with The Queen's Flight. A much-modified version, the Andover CC. Mk 1, is in RAF service as a tactical transport. Current production model, which superseded the Series 2 from mid-1967, is the Series 2A, which has an improved performance resulting from the installation of 2,280 ehp Dart RDa. 7 Mk 532–2L engines. The first Series 2A entered service with Varig of Brazil in August 1968.

12 **Fokker–VFW Friendship**
Probably the nearest approach to the elusive 'DC-3 replacement' is the Fokker Friendship, whose steady sales during more than a dozen years have established it as the world's biggest-selling turboprop-powered commercial transport by a handsome margin. Design studies for the F.27, Fokker's first airliner since the 1930s, were initiated in 1950, and after study of a variety of configurations a decision was made in favour of a twin-Dart aeroplane with pressurised accommodation for 28 passengers and a minimum range of 300 miles (483 km) with a capacity payload. Like the pre-war Fokkers, the new design, named Friendship, favoured a high wing layout, and the first of the two flying prototypes, PH-NIV, flew for the first time on 24 November 1955, powered by Dart Mk 507 turboprops. The second and subsequent

Friendships were 3 ft 0 in (0·91 m) longer, permitting four more passengers to be carried, and the higher-powered Dart Mk 528 was selected for the initial production version. In April 1956 the Dutch manufacturer signed an agreement with Fairchild, which had been building Fokker trainers in the United States for several years, to build and market the Friendship on that side of the Atlantic. The first Fairchild machine (N1027) was flown on 12 April 1958. Production Friendships built in Holland are identified by Mark numbers, and those from Fairchild (now Fairchild Hiller) by F-27 or FH-227 designations. The first and basic 44-seat production model was the Mk 100 (= F-27), which entered service with West Coast Airlines (F-27) in September and with Aer Lingus (Friendship Mk 100) in December 1958. This was followed by the Mk 200 (= F-27A), generally similar but with 2,050 shp Dart RDa. 7 Mk 532-7 engines. The Mk 300 (= F-27B) was a Fairchild-developed passenger/cargo version of the Mk 100 with reinforced floor and a large portside freight door, and the Mk 400 Combiplane a similar counterpart, by Fokker only, of the Mk 200. Fokker was responsible for the Mk 400M Troopship, a military troop- and freight-carrier version of the 200 in service with the Royal Netherlands Air Force, Argentine Air Force and Sudan Air Force, and also for the first stretched version, the Mk 500, which has a 4 ft 11 in (1·50 m) longer fuselage, freight-loading door, Dart 528's and space for 52 passengers. The Mk 600 is a cargo version of the Mk 200, with optional quick-change capability. Fairchild developments include the F-27F and F-27J business variants, with Dart Mk 529 and 532 engines respectively, and the high-altitude F-27M. After the amalgamation with Hiller Aircraft in 1964 the American manufacturer produced its own stretched versions in the FH-227, FH-227B, C, D and E, which are 52-seaters, 6 ft 6 in (1·98 m) longer than the F-27 and powered by Dart Mk 532's. The first FH-227 flew in March 1966 and was delivered to Mohawk Airlines during the following month. By June 1971, five hundred and seventy-three Friendships had been ordered, of which four hundred and forty-three were for airline customers. American production (total one hundred and ninety-eight) has now ended, but Dutch production was continuing in 1971.

13 Antonov An-24 ('Coke')

Even without the high wing layout that has become a regular feature of Antonov designs, the An-24 would obviously bear close comparison with such western counterparts as the Friendship and the Herald. It is particularly comparable to the Friendship, being nearly identical in terms of overall size, weight and general performance; the chief point of difference is the Russian aeroplane's shorter range. However, the An-24 was intended for short-stage local service routes between communities with only second-class or unprepared airfields – hence the rather high available power and the high wing position, which has the added advantage of minimising the risk of propeller damage while using such strips. Design of the An-24 was begun, after discussions with Aeroflot in the spring of 1958, to provide the Soviet state airline with a 32/40-seat short-hauler to replace its veteran piston-engined Il-14's and Li-2's. The first of two prototypes ('CCCP-1959') was flown for the first time at Kiev at the end of April 1960, by test pilot G. Lysenko. Several modifications were apparent in the second machine, 'CCCP-1960', when it appeared later that year. Among these were an extended fuselage nose, elongated engine nacelles, a dorsal fin and additional fin area under the tail cone. This external configuration has remained basically unaltered, though internal rearrangement has increased the seating capacity of the An-24V first to 44 and then, in the Series II which has been the standard passenger version since 1968, to 50. A flight crew of up to five can be carried. Two static-test aircraft and three pre-series machines were built before the An-24V entered regular production in 1962. The early aircraft were subjected to typically thorough flight test and route-proving programmes before, in September 1963, Aeroflot introduced the type on scheduled services from Moscow to Voronezh and Saratov. In 1964 the An-24V became available for export, and by 1971 the list of customers included Air Guinée, Air Mali, Balkan Bulgarian Airlines, Cubana, Inter-

flug, Lebanese Air Transport, LOT, Misrair, Mongolian Airlines, Pan African Air Services and Tarom.

The standard version in production in 1971–72 was the An-24V Series II, which has AI-24A water-injection engines and is available in mixed-traffic, convertible, all-cargo or executive versions in addition to the standard 50-seater. A variant known as the An-24RV has a 1,985 lb (900 kg) st Type RU 19-300 auxiliary turbojet engine in the rear of the starboard nacelle, to improve engine starting, take-off and in-flight performance.

14 Handley Page Herald

The Herald suffered somewhat from the decision to persevere, in the early stages, with a piston-engined version of the design. Handley Page's decision to proceed with a 44-seat feederliner was taken in the early 1950s. As the H.P.R.3, work began in 1954 to complete two prototypes, each powered by four Alvis Leonides piston engines. By the time that the first of these (G-AODE) made its maiden flight on 25 August 1955, Handley Page had received orders for nearly thirty Heralds from Queensland Airlines, Australian National Airlines and Lloyd Aero Columbiano, together with a provisional order from Air Kruise, and plans were well advanced to lay down a production line. By this time, however, the advent of the Friendship and Viscount had caused many operators to revise their attitude to turbine transports, and some Herald customers declined to accept it in piston-engined form.

As a result, Handley Page offered the twin-Dart H.P.R.7 as an alternative, this being basically the same design except for a slightly longer fuselage seating up to 44 people and modifications made necessary by the change of powerplant. In its new form, G-AODE made its second 'maiden' flight on 11 March 1958, followed on 17 December by the second Dart Herald, G-AODF. In June 1959 the first order for the new Herald was placed by the British government, who bought three Series 100 for use on the 'Highlands and Islands' services of BEA; and subsequent sales continued steadily if not spectacularly. Major production version was the Series 200, which is 3 ft 6 in (1·07 m) longer and seats up to 56 passengers. The Series 400 is a military freighter equivalent with reinforced flooring and side-loading doors. The three BEA Series 100's were sold to Autair in 1966; operators of the thirty-six Series 200's built included Air Manila, Alia (Jordan), Arkia (Israel), Bavaria Flug, BUIA, Eastern Provincial (Canada), Europe Aero Service, Far East Air Transport (Taiwan), Itavia (Italy) and Sadia (Brazil).

15 Aérospatiale N 262 and Frégate

The Nord 262 has been labelled as a 'DC-3 replacement', though in view of the number of earlier attempts to replace the apparently irreplaceable, such a tag might have been thought more of a hindrance than a help. Its origins date back to 1957 and the M.H. 250 Super Broussard

22-seat feederliner, a square-bodied, twin-engined aeroplane developed by Avions Max Holste after experience in operating the smaller single-engined Broussard general purpose aircraft. With two 600 hp Pratt & Whitney R-1340 piston engines, the M.H. 250 prototype flew on 20 May 1959, but further development was shelved in favour of the alternative M.H. 260, which was 4 ft 7 in (1·39 m) longer and powered by Turboméca Bastan turboprops. The first M.H. 260 (F-WJDV) flew on 29 July 1960 with two 805 ehp Bastan IIIA's, these giving way three months later to 986 ehp Bastan IV's. The French government provided financial assistance towards a first batch of ten M.H. 260's to be completed by Nord-Aviation, the first of which (F-WJSN) flew on 29 January 1962. However, no more than these ten were completed, for Nord had continued separately to develop the M.H. 262, which had more powerful Bastan VI engines and seated up to 29 passengers in a circular-section pressurised fuselage. It was this, as the Nord 262, which became the definitive design. The prototype flew on 24 December 1962, and the first of three pre-series machines in the following May. Air Inter became, in the summer of 1963, the first Nord 262 customer; pending delivery of these a number of M.H. 260's were acquired on lease and put into service immediately the 262 had received French type certification on 16 July 1964. The remaining M.H. 260's were lease-operated by Widerøe's Flyveselskap for a similar period. The first four production aircraft, for Air Inter, were designated Series B; production then continued with the Series A for other customers. The Nord 262 broke into the American market when, in June 1964, Lake Central Airlines confirmed an initial order for eight aircraft, but hopes of further American sales did not materialise. It entered service with Lake Central in mid-1965, following FAA type approval in March, but by mid-1971 total sales had reached only ninety-three aircraft, of which thirty-nine were for the French Air Force and Navy. In parallel production with the Series A is the Frégate, which is being built for civil customers as the Series C and the French Air Force as the Series D. The Frégate has more powerful (1,145 ehp) Bastan VII engines and raked tips to the wings and tailplane, the former for better performance at 'hot and high' airfields and the latter improving low-speed handling.

16 Saunders ST-27

One of the growing areas of air travel in recent years has been that of the third-level operators – those flying commuter and other local services – and the aircraft needs of these operators are thus a profitable subject of current study for aircraft designers and manufacturers. Low-budget operators flying short-stage routes at low-level fares are clearly not in the market for expensive or highly-sophisticated aeroplanes, and one way to meet their needs at minimum cost is to adapt an existing aircraft design to a more economical means of operation. One of the more attractive results of such an exercise is that evolved by David Saunders, of Saunders Aircraft Corporation, Montreal, whose ST-27 is basically a modernised development of the de Havilland Heron. The major outward changes are the replacement of the original four de Havilland Gipsy Queen piston-engines by a pair of PT6A turboprops, and the insertion of additional sections totalling 8 ft 6 in (2·59 m) in the fuselage, which permits the passenger accommodation to be increased from 17 to 24. Other changes include a 1 ft 6 in (0·46 m) longer nose-cone, re-shaped rudder and a redesigned wing structure; otherwise the wings, landing gear and tail assembly are essentially those of the retractable-undercarriage Heron Series 2. The prototype ST-27 (CF-YBM-X) was completed in England by Aviation Traders (Engineering) Ltd at Southend from a Heron 2 formerly belonging to The Queen's Flight. It made its first flight on 28 May 1969 and received a British C of A on 16 September 1970. By mid-1971 ST-27's had been ordered by three US customers and one Canadian; one had been completed and three others (converted from Queen's Flight Herons) were almost completed. Certification by the FAA and the Canadian Department of Transport was anticipated during 1971, to be followed by the first deliveries, to Air North of Burlington, Vermont, and Millard Air of Toronto. Saunders is also studying a design known as the ST-30, based on ST-27 technology and powered by PT6-34 engines.

17 Swearingen Metro

Of generally similar overall appearance to the Saunders ST-27 (see above), the 20-passenger Metro third-level/commuter transport is, however, an entirely new design. Swearingen Aircraft of San Antonio, Texas, is well known for its range of Merlin twin-engined business executive aircraft, and the SA-226TC Metro is in fact an outgrowth of the Merlin IIB/Merlin III; a 10/12-seat executive version of the Metro is known as the Merlin IV. The Metro prototype (N226TC) made its first flight on 26 August 1969, having been developed originally at the instigation of Fairchild Hiller. It carries a crew of 2 and can, if required, be converted easily to a cargo transport, carrying a 5,000 lb (2,268 kg) payload. Weather radar is mounted in the aircraft's nose.

The first customer delivery of a Metro was made to MIBA (Société Minère de Bakwanga) at Kinshasa, in the Congolese Republic, early in 1971, and in the spring of that year others were under construction for Texas International Airlines.

18 Let L-410 Turbolet

The Let National Corporation of Kunovice, Czechoslovakia, established in 1950, has in the past been responsible for manufacture of the Soviet Yak-11 trainer and the twin-engined Aero 45 air taxi, and is currently building the Z-37 Cmelák single-engined agricultural aeroplane. The twin-turboprop L-410 short-haul airliner programme, which was started in 1966, thus represents its biggest and most ambitious venture to date. Design was under the leadership of Ing Ladislav Smrcek, and details of the Turbolet were first announced in 1968, coinciding with the 50th anniversary of the Czechoslovak aircraft industry. The first of four prototypes (OK-YKE) made its maiden flight on 16 April 1969 on the power of two Canadian PT6A-27 turboprops, and these engines have also been fitted to subsequent prototypes. The original intention was that production aircraft should be powered by Czech-designed M 601 turboprop engines of 730 eshp, with the Canadian engines available optionally – primarily for the benefit of potential western customers, since the L-410 was intended to be sold to a wide international market. Since the Soviet invasion of Czechoslovakia in 1968 the continuing validity of these intentions has seemed less certain. Development of the M 601 has progressed only slowly, and by mid-1971 none of the intended batch of six pre-series L-410's was known to have flown with these engines. Thus it seemed likely that the initial production series, at least, would be PT6A-powered. The first operator was Slov-Air, a newly-formed Czechoslovak internal airline, although a Turbolet (reportedly the second production example) was displayed in CSA colours at the 1971 Paris Air Show. The high-wing configuration and the style of the landing gear speak of the rough-field capabilities of the Turbolet, which in its passenger transport form seats from 12 to 20 people, with a one- or two-man crew, in the non-pressurised fuselage. As an all-cargo aircraft, the L-410 can carry a 4,188 lb (1,900 kg) freight load; mixed-traffic, executive, survey, ambulance or training layouts are possible, and a ski landing gear will be available optionally.

19 De Havilland Canada DHC-6 Twin Otter

Design of the DHC-6 Twin Otter originated as a private venture, in the early months of 1964, following research flying carried out by a specially-modified DHC-3 Otter aircraft. The objective was to combine a carrying capacity somewhat greater than that of the single-engined Otter with the additional safety factor inherent in a twin-engined design, while at the same time retaining the first-class STOL performance and economy of operation that had characterised the company's earlier products. Production costs were kept down by using as many components as possible from the wings and fuselage of the DHC-3, and no small contribution to the Twin Otter's success has been made by the PT6A engine, the first turboprop to be manufactured in Canada. An initial pre-production batch of five Twin Otters was started at Downsview, and the first of these (CF-DHC-X) made its first flight on 20 May 1965. This and the next three aircraft were

each powered by two 579 eshp PT6A-6 engines, but subsequent aircraft adopted as standard the PT6A-20 engine of the same power. To begin with, the Twin Otter was envisaged as a 15-passenger aircraft, but standard accommodation in the Series 100, as the initial production model became known, was increased to 18. The first one hundred and fifteen aircraft were completed as Series 100's. FAA type certification, granted in mid-1966, was quickly followed by the first customer delivery, to the Ontario Department of Lands and Forests. First exports, to the Fuerza Aérea de Chile, were made before the end of the year.

In April 1968, DHC introduced the Series 200 on to the production line. This was essentially similar to the original model, except for a much-increased baggage capacity achieved by extending the aft baggage compartment further into the rear of the fuselage and by lengthening the nose by 2 ft 3 in (0·68 m). An identical number of Series 200 Twin Otters were built before, in 1969, this model was in turn superseded by the Series 300, offering improved operating characteristics by combining the Series 200 airframe with more powerful 652 eshp PT6A-27 engines. The Series 300 was still in current production in the spring of 1971, by which time total sales of the Twin Otter had reached three hundred and thirty, of which three hundred had then been delivered. These are in service in every part of the world as passenger and/or cargo aircraft with several third-level operators or on a variety of other duties which include police, forestry or fishery patrol, Antarctic and other geophysical surveys, troop or paratroop transport, casualty evacuation, and search and rescue. The largest single operator of Twin Otters is Golden West Airlines of Los Angeles, which in 1971 had a fleet of more than thirty of these aircraft. Others are included in the fleets of such major airline operators as Aeronaves de Mexico, Ansett/MAL, East African, Guyana, Pakistan International, Sudan and Trans-Australia. Military operators include all three services in the Argentine, which have nine, and the air forces of Canada (eight), Chile (seven), Jamaica (one), Norway (four), Paraguay (one), Panama (one) and Peru (eleven). The Canadian Armed Forces' aircraft are designated CC-138. Another valuable service performed by Twin Otters is that of water-bombing in forest fire areas, the water load being carried either in specially-designed twin floats or, in the landplane, in an expendable membrane tank fitted under the fuselage. When fitted with floats the Twin Otter must also have the short nose (irrespective of Series number) and be fitted with wing fences and auxiliary tail fins.

20 Junkers Ju 52/3m

Nearly five thousand Ju 52/3m's were built in Germany during a production life spanning eleven years, and nearly two-thirds of this number was made up of those completed during World War 2 for use by the Luftwaffe on a variety of transport duties. There were many variants of this 'European DC-3', but all were basically similar airframes, the principal variation being the type of powerplant installed. These were nearly all radial-type engines, including the Pratt & Whitney Hornet, Wright Cyclone, BMW 132, Bristol Jupiter and Pegasus, Armstrong Siddeley Panther and Gnome-Rhône 9-Kbr; the Junkers Jumo 5 inline engine was also fitted successfully to some aircraft. The characteristic corrugated-metal skinning was a typical trade mark of Junkers aircraft of the 1920s and 1930s, and was designed to give great structural strength and resistance to torsional loads. Other unmistakable recognition features of the Ju 52/3m included the Junkers double flaps and elevators, and the toeing-out of the two wing-mounted engines. A substantial number of ex-Luftwaffe Ju 52/3m's became spoils of war after VE-day, and were employed in Europe as stop-gap airline equipment for the next two or three years. There were also a hundred and seventy CASA-built aircraft, and more than four hundred were completed in France by the Ateliers Aéronautiques de Colombes as the AAC. 1. In the immediate post-war years, Ju 52/3m's were in service with commercial operators in Norway, Sweden and Denmark; ten others, converted by Short & Harland Ltd, were employed by BEA until August 1947. The Ju 52/3m was most numerous, however, in France, being supplied to several domestic operators and to the national carrier, Air France, which at one time had a fleet of eighty-five of these veteran aircraft. Some of the Scandinavian machines were later sold to customers in Spain and elsewhere. The Ju 52/3m is now virtually extinct in both a military and a civil capacity, but one was still believed to be in service with Transportes Aéreos Orientales of Ecuador in 1971.

21 Britten-Norman Islander and Trislander

The partnership formed in 1952 between John Britten and Desmond Norman made its first major impact in aviation circles with an aerial crop-spraying service, but in recent years this has been overshadowed by the remarkable success of its second fixed-wing aircraft design, the BN-2 Islander. In November 1963, having seen a gap in the market for an extremely cheap feeder/charter aircraft – a latter-day Dragon Rapide, in effect – Britten-Norman began work on such a design. The first prototype (G-ATCT), completed with a little assistance from F. G. Miles and Westland Aircraft, was flown for the first time on 13 June 1965 with two Rolls-Royce/Continental IO-360 engines and a 45 ft 0 in (13·72 m) wing span. The original engines failed to realise their promised 210 hp each, and were replaced by 260 hp Lycoming O-540 engines. These, and a 49 ft 0 in (14·94 m) wing span, became standard features, and when the Islander appeared at the 1966

Biggin Hill Air Fair its STOL capabilities were dramatically demonstrated by a take-off accomplished within the length of the runway threshold markings. This followed a public début at the 1965 Paris Air Show and the collection, by the end of that year, of orders for more than thirty Islanders. By the time of the 1971 Paris Show that total had been increased tenfold, representing 120 operators in more than 50 countries – a tribute not only to the Islander's performance but to an equally attractive price. A British C of A was granted on 10 August 1967, followed on 19 December 1967 by FAA type approval. To cope with the fast-rising order list, Britten-Norman sub-contracted the manufacture of two hundred and thirty-six Islanders to the British Hovercraft Corporation, and in 1968 a licence agreement was concluded with the IRMA (Intreprinderea de Reparat Material Aeronautic) organisation in Romania, which is to build two hundred and fifteen by 1974. The first Romanian-built Islander was flown on 4 August 1969. The first Islander operator was Loganair of Scotland, to whose inter-island services the aircraft was ideally suited – a fact echoed in later years by Aurigny Air Services which, with a fleet of eight on Channel Island operations, has been one of the major Islander customers. Initial production aircraft were designated Series 1; they were superseded from mid-1969 by the BN-2A Series 2 with a side-loading baggage facility and detail equipment and aerodynamic improvements. Islander variants currently available in 1971 included one with 300 hp IO-540-K fuel-injection engines (for 'hot and high' operations with somewhat reduced payload) and another with 270 hp Lycoming TIO-540-H turbocharged engines. An optional fit on all models is Britten-Norman's 'Speedpak' modification, consisting of wingtip extensions, with raked-back tips, which contain an extra 49 Imp gallons (223 litres) of fuel and increase the overall span to 53 ft 0 in (16·15 m). Preliminary studies were being conducted in 1971 for a water-borne version of the aircraft known as the Sealander.

In the *Private Aircraft since 1946* volume in this series, in which the Islander was originally described and illustrated, reference was made to the 'stretch potential' of the basic design. This became fact in 1970, when on 11 September the first flight was made of the BN-2A Mk III, subsequently named Trislander. This has 'Speedpak' wings, a 7 ft 6 in (2·29 m) longer fuselage than the standard BN-2A, enabling the maximum passenger seating to be increased from 9 to 17, and three 260 hp O-540-E engines, the third one being mounted as an integral part of the modified vertical tail. British certification of the Trislander was granted on 14 May 1971, and by the end of May orders had been received for twenty-five examples of what one contemporary report has described as 'the twopenny Trident'. The first customer for the Trislander was Aurigny Air Services, whose first aircraft (of an initial order for

three) was delivered on 29 June 1971. A receiver to the Britten-Norman company was appointed in October 1971, at which time the future of the Trislander remained to be decided.

22 Avro Lancastrian

The first transport conversion of the celebrated Lancaster bomber was carried out in 1943 on behalf of Trans-Canada Air Lines. This aircraft was converted by A. V. Roe from a British-built bomber and, as CF-CMS, inaugurated a trans-Atlantic mail and VIP transport service on behalf of the Canadian government on 22 July 1943. During the following year a rather less elegant Lancaster conversion, with the nose and tail turrets crudely faired over, was flown as G-AGJI in BOAC colours as a testbed for new equipment intended for the Avro Tudor 1. Altogether, nineteen Lancaster transports of a similar kind appeared on the British register, although five of them served only to provide spares for the other fourteen. British South American Airways operated four long-nosed Lancasters for a time from 1946, and Skyways and Alitalia each acquired one as a crew trainer, but little other use was made of this rough Lancaster conversion. More widely employed as an interim airliner in the immediate post-war years was the Avro 691 Lancastrian; this, like the earlier CF-CMS, was characterised by streamlined nose and tail cones, the nose cone in this case being rather longer than that of the original machine. Again it was

TCA who set the ball rolling, by ordering twelve Lancastrian conversions (with 1,250 hp Packard-built Merlin 38 engines and seating for 10 passengers) from Victory Aircraft of Toronto. The first of these (CF-CMV) was delivered in 1945, and a similar adaptation (with 1,640 hp Merlin 24's) was embarked upon by the parent company. British-built Lancastrians were produced to both civil and military orders, the RAF receiving sixty-five Mks II and IV from October 1945 to meet the requirements of Air Ministry Specification C. 16/44. These were respectively 9- and 13-passenger aircraft, whose commercial counterparts were BOAC's Mk I and the Mk III for British South American Airways. The first Avro-built Lancastrian was G-AGLF (formerly Lancaster VB763), which was used to obtain the type's Certificate of Airworthiness early in 1945; G-AGLS was the first of an initial twenty for BOAC, with which scheduled services were initiated on 31 May 1945. In addition to the North Atlantic route, BOAC flew its Lancastrians on the 'Kangaroo' service to Australasia in collaboration with Qantas. In 1946 the larger-capacity Lancastrian III's of BSAA opened services to Buenos Aires and other points in South America; other Lancastrians saw service in the fleets of Alitalia, Silver City and Skyways. The Lancastrian was the first British commercial type physically capable of crossing the South Atlantic, and both in this and in the reduction of England–Australia travelling time

(to three days) it had no small prestige value at the time, despite its modest carrying capacity. But it was far from making economic sense on any route, and by 1947–48 had been relegated to hack transport work and the carriage of liquids in bulk, milk and petroleum in particular. It accepted its share of the work of the Berlin airlift in 1949 – as did some Lancaster transports too – but by the end of the decade had disappeared from service, and the last Lancastrians were reduced to scrap in 1951.

23 Handley Page Halifax and Halton

After the end of World War 2, as an interim step until genuine transport designs became established, each of Britain's two principal wartime bombers underwent somewhat rough-and-ready adaptation to provide cargo- and passenger-carrying facilities over ranges beyond the capacity of the smaller American C-46's and C-47's. The Lancaster-turned-Lancastrian was the more successful of the two, but some years of useful service were also given by adaptations of the Halifax. During what remained of the 1940s, one hundred and forty-seven Halifaxes appeared on the British civil register as passenger and/or cargo carriers, these comprising two B. III's, thirty-four B. VI's, seventy-nine C. VIII's and thirty-two A. IX's. The first of these 'civilianisations' was G-AGXA *Waltzing Matilda*, converted from a B. III bomber early in 1946 and demonstrated (and ultimately sold) in Australia. Further bomber conversions followed, being joined later by civil counterparts of the military Halifax transports. The large ventral freight pannier of these aircraft, capable of holding an 8,000 lb (3,630 kg) payload, made it particularly useful as a cargo aeroplane, although the fuselage provided seating accommodation for 10 passengers as well. Two of the largest fleets of Halifax transports and Haltons were operated by the Lancashire Aircraft Company and LAMS (London Aero and Motor Services). The LAMS Halifaxes operated chiefly to Australia and New Zealand, and many others were flown by small charter operators in Britain and Europe. Whereas the Halifax transport involved the minimum of adaptation necessary for civilian operation, a more serious attempt was made with its stablemate, the Halton, to restyle the aeroplane for commercial service. The Halton 1, twelve of which were produced, was adapted from the Halifax C. VIII to provide BOAC with a fleet of long-range transports to bridge the gap created by the development delays affecting the Avro Tudor. Externally, the principal differences noticeable were the larger passenger entrance door and the rectangular passenger cabin windows. The first Halton 1, G-AHDU *Falkirk*, was delivered to BOAC in July 1946, and Halton services began soon afterwards to West Africa, Cairo and Karachi. The Halton illustrated was the one and only Halton 2 which, after a short period of operation in the United Kingdom on behalf of the Maharajah of Baroda, ended its days in South Africa. By the end of 1947, BOAC had begun to replace its Haltons with Canadair DC-4M's, and by mid-1948 the decline in freight traffic appeared to have marked the end of the Halifax/Halton's usefulness. A temporary respite was afforded by the Berlin airlift, during which forty-one of these aircraft flew over eight thousand sorties with diesel fuel and dry cargo; but when the emergency ended in August 1949 the days of the surviving machines were indeed numbered, and by the end of the decade nearly all of them had been reduced to scrap.

24 Bristol Brabazon

One of the biggest and most ambitious projects ever attempted by the British aircraft industry, the Bristol Type 167 Brabazon was, technologically, far ahead of its time. Its development costs were therefore naturally high; as a consequence, it was a political embarrassment for virtually the whole of its eight-year career before the one and only completed aircraft went to the breakers after amassing less than four hundred hours flying in four years. The design originally submitted by Bristol was to meet the requirement – for a high-speed, high-capacity airliner capable of crossing the Atlantic non-stop – that later crystallised as the Brabazon Committee's Type I. It was based on the company's proposals, formulated in 1942, for a butterfly-tailed one-hundred-ton bomber. In May 1943 Bristol received a letter of intent covering two prototypes and up to ten production aircraft, so long as this did not affect war production. Various body configurations were studied during the ensuing year and a half, and by November 1944 the basic design had been established sufficiently for construction of a mock-up to begin. A conventional tail assembly was now proposed, and the powerplant was to consist of eight Centaurus radial piston engines, completely enclosed in the wings and geared in pairs to drive contra-rotating propellers. In October 1945 construction of the first prototype began. The sheer size of the venture posed many problems – intrinsic ones, such as pressurising a fuselage of some 25,000 cu ft (708 m³) capacity, and associated ones like the erection of an 8-acre (3·24 hectare) final assembly shed. The necessity to extend and strengthen the Filton runway involved demolishing part of a nearby village and closing a new by-pass road; and, combined with a thorough programme of stress tests at Filton and the Royal Aircraft Establishment, served to defer the first flight by G-AGPW until 4 September 1949. This machine was intended to serve only as a flight test aircraft, but during 1950 thirty seats were installed in the rear passenger cabin for demonstration flight purposes. It was the intention to develop the Brabazon Mk I as a 72/80-seater for BOAC's North Atlantic services. The Brabazon Mk II was to have been a 100-seater with four 7,000 ehp Coupled-Proteus 710 turboprops, but this version was shelved in

1952 before the second prototype (which would have served as the development aircraft) was fully completed. The Brabazon's unhappy career was then nearly at an end. True, much was learned while building and flying it that benefited the Britannia and other Bristol designs; but the belief remains that, when G-AGPW was reduced to scrap in October 1953, a potentially great aeroplane had been sacrificed for political reasons rather than technological failings.

25 Avro Tudor

When the Avro Tudor 1 prototype G-AGPF took off from Ringway Airport for its maiden flight on 14 June 1945, it seemed to embody every ingredient for success. Its handsome lines would undoubtedly appeal to passengers; its pressurised fuselage was the first on any British transport; and its wings, based on those of the Lincoln bomber, carried four Rolls-Royce Merlins, among the most reliable engines in the world. Yet the Tudor's unfortunate career was one of modification, changing customer requirements and support, failure to achieve its design performance and several serious accidents. There were two basic Tudors, the design of which was started in mid-1944. The Avro 688 was represented by the short-fuselage Tudors 1, 3 and 4; while the Avro 689 (Tudors 2, 5 and 7) featured a fuselage 1 ft (0·30 m) greater in diameter and ultimately lengthened by 26 ft 1 in (7·95 m). The most noticeable outward revisions of the Tudor 1 design were the longer inboard nacelles of the Merlin 621 engines (the prototype had Merlin 102A's) and the much-enlarged tail assembly. The Tudor 2 prototype, G-AGSU, also underwent similar modification after its first flight on 10 March 1946. In April 1947, two years after ordering twenty-two of the 24-seat Tudor 1's, BOAC decided that the aircraft was not suited to the North Atlantic and cancelled its order. It had also ordered seventy-nine 60-seat Tudor 2's, with a view to operating them in pool with Qantas and South African Airways on the Empire routes; but when the latter version proved overweight and underpowered, this order too was reduced until BOAC abandoned interest in the Tudor altogether. The experiment of fitting 1,715 hp Hercules 120 radial engines to G-AGRX, the first production Tudor 2 (making it the sole Tudor 7) proved unsuccessful; and the crash of G-AGSU on 23 August 1947 in which the Tudor's designer, Roy Chadwick, was among those killed, dealt a further blow to the aeroplane's prospects. Of the production Tudor 1's laid down, two were completed for the Ministry of Supply as 9-seat Tudor 3 official transports, and it was planned to complete the remainder for British South American Airways as 32-seat Tudor 4's or 4B's with a 6 ft (1·83 m) longer fuselage. Six were delivered to BSAA, but the early loss of two in crashes led to the remainder being relegated to a freight-only role. Five Tudor 5's (44-seat conversions of the Tudor 2) for BSAA were also

withheld from passenger service. The Berlin airlift saw several Tudor 4, 4B or 5 aircraft in service as freighters or tankers. These were withdrawn after the emergency, but in 1952 about a dozen Tudors, mostly 4B's, were given a new lease of life by Aviation Traders Ltd, who re-engined them with Merlin 623's, fitting out some with 42-seat interiors and others (as Super Trader 4B's) for cargo duties. A new C of A was granted early in 1954, and for several years the modified Tudors were employed by Air Charter on passenger flights to West Africa and on long range trooping or commercial charters. Air Charter maintained its small fleet for some years, but by the end of 1960 there were no longer any Tudors in regular service.

26 Handley Page Hermes

The Hermes was the first new British aircraft built after the war to go into service with British Overseas Airways Corporation, although the design had its origins in a specification for a 34/50-passenger airliner issued in 1944. An early project, based largely on Halifax components and known as the H.P. 64, was dropped in favour of the single-finned H.P. 68 Hermes 1. The latter was powered by 1,650 hp Bristol Hercules 101 engines and featured a pressurised passenger cabin. Development of the Hermes received a serious setback when the first prototype (G-AGSS) crashed on taking off for its maiden flight on 3 December 1945, and attention was for a time diverted to its military counterpart, the RAF Hastings, whose prototype (TE580) was flown successfully on 7 May 1946. However, following an order in April 1947 for twenty-five production Hermes airliners for BOAC, a second development aircraft was flown for the first time on 2 September 1947. This was G-AGUB, the sole H.P. 74 Hermes 2, which had a 15 ft 4 in (4·67 m) longer fuselage, 1,675 hp Hercules 121 engines and, like the Hermes 1, circular passenger windows and a tailwheel undercarriage. The definitive production model was the H.P. 81 Hermes 4, the first of which (G-AKFP) made its maiden flight on 5 September 1948. Among the changes noted in the production version were a nosewheel landing gear, rectangular windows and a significant increase in available power, the employment of 2,100 hp Hercules 763's permitting a maximum payload of 17,000 lb (7,711 kg) to be carried. The first Hermes 4 was delivered to BOAC on 2 February 1950, and the type entered service later that year on the Corporation's routes to West and South Africa. Normal complement was 40 passengers in addition to the five-man crew, although the Hermes was capable of seating as many as 63 people. The Hermes was meant only as an interim BOAC type, and its replacement by Canadair Argonauts began after only some two years of service. Among the first customers for the ex-BOAC aircraft was Airwork Ltd, who modified their machines to Hermes 4A's by fitting 2,125 hp Hercules 773's

before putting them to use as 68-seaters on military trooping charters. These were restored in 1957 to Mk 4 standard and, with other surviving Hermes 4's, served for the remainder of the 1950s and early 1960s with such British independents as Air Safaris, Falcon Airways, Skyways and Silver City. Two others were operated as 78-seaters by Bahamas Airways. Fifteen Hermes 4's were still active in 1960, but by the mid-1960s the type was no longer operational. Two other aircraft, H.P. 82 Hermes 5's, were completed in 1949–50 as turbine development aircraft with 2,490 ehp Bristol Theseus 502 turboprops, but no production of this version was undertaken.

27 Boeing Stratocruiser
The requirement for a transport development of the B-29 Superfortress bomber was first drawn up, in the middle years of World War 2, as a military one for Air Transport Command of the USAAF. To meet this need, Boeing produced the Model 367, or YC-97, which utilised the same wing, engines, landing gear and tail assembly as the B-29 in conjunction with a two-deck 'double-bubble' fuselage of great strength and capacity, and fully pressurised. The first YC-97 was flown on 9 October 1945, and nearly nine hundred military Strato-freighters (C-97's) and Strato-tankers (KC-97's) were subsequently completed. One of these was adapted as prototype for a post-war civil development, the Boeing 377, planned to carry 100 passengers

or a 35,000 lb (15,876 kg) payload over long ranges. This prototype was flown for the first time on 8 July 1947. The first customer for the Stratocruiser, as the civil version was named, was Pan American, who placed an order for twenty in June 1946; other orders followed from American Overseas Airlines (eight), Northwest (ten) and United Air Lines (seven) in the United States, and BOAC (six) and SAS (four) in Europe. In the event, the Stratocruiser did not serve with SAS, whose order was added to the original BOAC requirement. Production of the fifty-five came to an end in March 1950. The first Stratocruiser services were operated by Pan American, who put the type into service on 7 September 1948; BOAC began its Stratocruiser services on 6 December 1949. Pan American later increased its fleet to twenty-seven by purchase of the prototype and six of the AOA aircraft. Both its crews (normally comprising five men) and its passengers appreciated the spaciousness of the Stratocruiser's flight deck and passenger cabin, the latter including a lounge or cocktail bar on the lower deck at the rear of the generous luggage hold. The Stratocruiser could accommodate up to 89 passengers in a typical five-abreast tourist configuration, or up to 112 in a high-density layout, and its standards of comfort were scarcely bettered until the large-scale introduction of jets began in 1958. On 16 July 1958, one of the BOAC aircraft (which had been augmented by a further six aircraft purchased from United and one from Pan American) inaugurated services between London and Accra on behalf of the newly formed Ghana Airways Corporation; but by mid-1959 the British operator had withdrawn all its Stratocruisers from service. In 1960 about a score of Stratocruisers were still extant (mostly with Transocean), but by 1963 the type had disappeared completely from the commercial passenger scene.

28 **Douglas DC-4**

A contemporary of the DC-3, the original Douglas DC-4 began its evolution in mid-1935 to the requirement of a number of US domestic operators for a 52-passenger airliner for medium-stage lengths of up to 2,500 miles (4,023 km). Two prototypes to this specification were completed, the first (NX18100) flying for the first time on 7 June 1938 powered by four 1,150 hp Pratt & Whitney R-2180 Twin Hornet engines. This early DC-4, although certificated in May 1939, was rejected by the airlines, who felt that a smaller-capacity machine would be more viable economically; accordingly Douglas began work on a smaller single-finned design (the first DC-4 had a triple tail unit) seating up to 42 passengers. American, Eastern and United placed orders for the smaller version totalling sixty-one aircraft, but by the time that the prototype flew on 14 February 1942 the United States was committed in World War 2, and all transport aircraft in production, the DC-4 included, were diverted to the US armed services.

Large numbers of DC-4's were built during the war as C-54 and R5D Skymasters, and by the time production finally ceased in August 1947 a total of one thousand and eighty-four Skymasters and seventy-nine civil DC-4's had been completed. A substantial number of surplus Skymasters joined the post-war DC-4's on the civil market, and became one of the standard types used to re-equip leading international airlines in the early years until the appearance of post-war designs. There were still nearly two hundred DC-4's in commercial service in 1970; they have a seating capacity ranging from 44 to 86 passengers according to layout, but most of them are now doing duty as freighters with appropriate modifications which include strengthened floors and large cargo doors in the side. Twenty-three were converted by Aviation Traders as ATL. 98 Carvair freighters; this conversion is described separately on page 133. Another DC-4 variant was the 40/55-seat Canadian conversion known as the North Star. This was first produced by Canadair for the RCAF, and comprised twenty-three C-54G's, fitted with 1,740 hp Rolls-Royce Merlin 620 engines and embodying appropriate structural changes. Six of these were loaned to Trans-Canada Airlines, these being unpressurised aircraft bearing the civil designation DC-4M-1. They were put into service in April 1947, but returned to the RCAF in the following year. Their place was taken by twenty DC-4M-2's, incorporating a number of features of

the DC-6 including pressurisation and square passenger cabin windows. These aircraft commenced trans-Atlantic operation with TCA in April 1948. Following its disenchantment with the Avro Tudor, BOAC ordered a fleet of twenty-two DC-4M-2's in 1948 which it put into service (to the Far East) from August 1949 under the class name Argonaut. In the late 1950s this fleet was sold off to BOAC associates or independent airlines, with whom they continued in operation until the late 1960s.

29 Douglas DC-6 series

Design of the DC-6 actually began to military requirements during World War 2 for a 'heavy' development of the C-54 Skymaster (DC-4), and the first aircraft of this type to fly, on 15 February 1946, was an XC-112A ordered by the USAAF. Aircraft of the DC-6 type did indeed serve with the US forces, but it is as a civil transport that the aeroplane is generally known. Unlike its predecessor, the DC-6 had a pressurised cabin accommodating up to 68 passengers in addition to the crew of three and was 6 ft 8 in (2·03 m) longer than the DC-4. Other improvements included more powerful engines, large square passenger windows and revision of the wing and tail areas. Among the first domestic carriers to be interested in the DC-6 was United Air Lines, which placed an order for thirty-five aircraft, and American Airlines, which ordered forty-seven. Production deliveries began early in 1947 to United, which put the type into operation across the United States in April of that year. First European delivery was OO-AWA, made to the Belgian airline Sabena three months later, and other European recipients included KLM and SAS. Altogether, one hundred and seventy-five DC-6's were built, these being succeeded by seventy-seven DC-6A's, a freight development which first flew on 29 September 1949 and entered service in 1951. Five feet (1·52 m) longer than the DC-6, the DC-6A incorporated cargo-loading doors, a strengthened fuselage floor and -CB17 engines. Payload was considerably better than that of the DC-6, and some DC-6A's were converted to DC-6C passenger or cargo aircraft with a maximum seating, in the former role, for 107 people. Major production of DC-6A's, however, concerned one hundred and sixty-seven C-118 or R6D Liftmasters for the US Air Force and Navy. The variant produced in greatest numbers for the civil market was the DC-6B, which flew for the first time on 10 February 1951 and began to be delivered (starting with Western Airlines) in April. With a further 1 ft 1 in (0·33 m) extension to the fuselage, the DC-6B was otherwise a passenger-carrying equivalent of the DC-6A and -6C, having maximum accommodation for 107 passengers or a payload nearly half as great again as the original DC-6. Two hundred and eighty-six DC-6B's were built for commercial customers before its production, and that of the entire DC-6 series, came to an end late in

1958. The DC-6B has proved that it has excellent operating economics, and well over two hundred DC-6 variants of one kind or another were still in airline service at the start of 1970.

30 Douglas DC-7 series

The DC-7 was the outcome of an approach to Douglas by American Airlines in 1951 to produce a stretched version of the DC-6B, with which American hoped to counter the introduction by TWA of the Super Constellation on domestic trunk routes. Douglas met this requirement by extending the DC-6B fuselage by 2 ft 3 in (0·69 m) to make it a 69/95-seater, and making use for the first time in the DC-4/DC-6 line of development of the Wright Turbo Compound engine. Four R-3350-988-TC18-DA4 engines, each of 3,250 hp, were installed in the prototype DC-7, which flew for the first time on 18 May 1953. In terms of capacity, the DC-7 compared well with the DC-6B, gross weight being increased to 122,200 lb (55,429 kg) and maximum payload to 20,000 lb (9,072 kg); but in operation it proved to be less economical, and engine vibration and noise levels were excessive by comparison. Nevertheless, one hundred and twenty DC-7's were built. In addition, Douglas completed ninety-seven DC-7B's, an essentially similar version for overseas routes which flew on 25 April 1955 and entered service (with Pan American) in the following month. The DC-7B retained the powerplant and seating capacity of the DC-7, differing principally in the additional fuel tankage necessary for long-range flying. Maximum take-off weight was increased to 126,000 lb (57,152 kg) and payload to 21,516 lb (9,759 kg). However, the DC-7B still did not have the truly intercontinental range demanded by such operators as PanAm, and to try and provide this capability Douglas embarked upon a further programme of modifying and stretching which resulted in the DC-7C. This model made its maiden flight on 20 December 1955 and was the first to make effective use of the Turbo Compound engine. The problems of finding additional fuel storage and reducing the cabin noise level were met by the single step of inserting an additional 5 ft 0 in (1·52 m) of wing between the fuselage and each inboard nacelle. Flap and aileron area was increased, and the more powerful -EA4 version of the Wright engine adopted as powerplant. The fuselage was extended a further 3 ft 4 in, seating up to 105 passengers, and fin and rudder areas were increased. Other aerodynamic improvements were made, and up-to-date weather radar, de-icing and other equipment fitted. Thus improved, the DC-7C had a better airfield performance than any of its forebears, despite an all-up weight now as high as 143,000 lb (64,863 kg) which included a 25,350 lb (10,592 kg) payload. Moreover, it could achieve ranges in excess of 4,000 miles (6,437 km) with such loads. Production of the DC-7 series ended late in 1958 after

the completion of three hundred and thirty-eight aircraft, one hundred and twenty-one of these being DC-7C's. Since 1959 a number of operators have had their DC-7's or -7C's converted to DC-7F all-freight aircraft. At the beginning of 1970 some seventy-five DC-7 series aircraft were still in airline operation.

31   SIAI-Marchetti S.M.95

The S.M. 95 actually began life as a war transport, the first prototype making its maiden flight on 8 May 1943, before the Italian surrender, on the power of four 850 hp Alfa Romeo 131 RC 14/50 radial engines. This powerplant was later replaced by Alfa Romeo 128 RC 18 radials, which also powered the two other S.M. 95's completed, by SAI Ambrosini at Perugia, before the end of the war in Europe. These were medium-range 18-seaters, with a 73 ft 0 in (22·25 m) fuselage, gross weight of 46,297 lb (21,000 kg) and a range of 1,243 miles (2,000 km), carrying a flight crew of four or five. After the war the design was enlarged to enable the S.M. 95 to operate over shorter stage lengths carrying up to 38 passengers in a fuselage lengthened to 81 ft 3¼ in (24·77 m). Despite the S.M. 95's good handling qualities, production of the civil version was extremely limited, and probably totalled little more than a dozen aircraft. The post-war production S.M. 95's were delivered either with Alfa Romeo 128 engines, with 920 hp Bristol Pegasus 48's, or with 1,065 hp Pratt & Whitney R-1830-S13CG's. Six S.M. 95's were delivered to the Italian national carrier, Alitalia, with whom they entered service in April 1948. Alitalia also acquired three Twin-Wasp-engined S.M. 95's (its own having been Pegasus-powered), and continued to operate the type until 1951. Three S.M. 95's were also operated by SAIDE of Egypt. One of the wartime trio operated for a while in 1945–46 between Great Britain and the Continent bearing post-war Italian Air Force insignia.

32 Sud-Est Languedoc

The origins of this post-war French airliner are to be found in the 12-passenger M.B. 160 evolved for Air Afrique in 1937 by Marcel Bloch (now Marcel Dassault). Powered by four 720 hp Hispano-Suiza 12 Xirs engines, the M.B. 160 set up two speed-with-payload records late in 1937, but it did not enter production. In its place Bloch developed the M.B. 161, a parallel design to the M.B. 162 heavy bomber, as a 33-seat passenger airliner tailored to the needs of Air France for operation over medium stage lengths. The 'MB' was retained in the designation despite the Bloch organisation's absorption in the nationalised SNCA du Sud-Ouest in January 1937, and a prototype of the M.B. 161 (F-ARTV) was flown for the first time in September 1939. After the fall of France, continued development of the aeroplane was authorised by the Vichy government, and preparations were made to begin production in 1941 at the SNCA du Sud-Est factory at Toulouse, to meet a German order for the completion of twenty aircraft. The

prototype resumed test flying in 1942, and was later used as a VIP transport, but no production aircraft were completed until after the liberation. The first Toulouse-built S.E. 161 Languedoc (as the type then became known) was flown on 17 September 1945, with the registration F-BATA and a power-plant of four 1,150 hp Gnome-Rhône 14N 44/45 engines. Forty Languedocs were ordered by Air France for its European and North African services, and other operators included Air Atlas, Air Liban, Iberia, Misrair, LOT and Tunis Air. Initially it was planned to power the production Languedoc with Gnome-Rhône engines, but these did not prove entirely satisfactory and the standard engine on most of the one hundred machines completed became the 1,200 hp Pratt & Whitney R-1830-S1C3-G. The Languedoc's fuselage, although long, had a narrower internal cabin width than the DC-3, and the 33 passengers were accommodated in three-abreast seating; the payload capacity was 8,650 lb (3,924 kg). Several Languedocs were supplied to the Armée de l'Air and Aéronavale, the latter force still retaining a few for aircrew training as late as 1960. By that time Aviaco of Spain, with a fleet of five, was the sole remaining civil operator of the Languedoc, and the type is no longer in commercial use. A number of Languedocs were used during the late 1940s as flying testbeds for aero-engines and other devices; among these were four aircraft employed as carriers for the Leduc series of ramjet research vehicles which were mounted, pick-a-back fashion, above the Languedoc fuselage.

33   Handley Page Marathon

As the M. 60, the Marathon was designed by Miles Aircraft Ltd to Specification 18/44 to meet the Type VA requirement of the Brabazon Committee for a feeder-liner for the British internal route network. Originally registered U-10, and later G-AGPD, the first of three 14/18-seat prototypes ordered was completed in fourteen months and made a successful maiden flight on 19 May 1946, powered by four 330 hp Gipsy Queen 71 engines. This, like the production aircraft, featured a triple-tail assembly, though the second prototype (G-AILH, first flown on 27 February 1947) was given only twin fins and rudders for comparative purposes. In 1948, Miles Aircraft went into liquidation, the company's remaining assets being taken over by Handley Page in June. Renamed as Handley Page (Reading) Ltd, the former Miles factory continued development of the Marathon under the new designation H.P.R. 1. Forty production Marathon 1's were at this time on order for British European Airways, and the first production Marathon (G-ALUB) was used on proving flights in 1951. But the airline decided that the Marathon did not fully meet its requirements; and finally, in 1952, it secured government approval to withdraw the order. The Royal Air Force, after evaluating two Marathon 1's from 1951, took a further twenty-eight converted as T. 11 advanced navigation trainers. Of the remainder of the final total of forty-three Marathons built, including prototypes, six (of a total of eight completed originally for BEA) were supplied to West African Airways Corporation in 1952, three to Union of Burma Airways, two to Far East Airlines (Japan) and one in 1954 to King Hussein of Jordan as a VIP transport. Powerplant of the standard Marathon 1 was four 340 hp Gipsy Queen 70-3 engines, but those in WAAC service were re-engined with Gipsy Queen 70-4's of similar power and designated Marathon 1A. Seating capacity of the Marathon was for up to 22 passengers, and maximum payload was 5,036 lb (2,284 kg). In 1954 the West African machines were returned to Britain, where, in subsequent times, the principal operator was Derby Aviation; but none now remain in service. The Marathon's high-wing layout and roomy fuselage made it popular with its passengers, and Miles-designed high-lift flaps gave it a creditable short-field performance for its time. The third prototype Marathon to be completed, G-AHXU, was a development aircraft for the proposed M 69. Marathon 2, and was powered by two 1,010 ehp Armstrong Siddeley Mamba 502 turboprops. This aircraft flew for the first time on 23 July 1949, but no production of a turbine-engined version was undertaken. This prototype became, in 1955, an engine and nacelle testbed for the Leonides Major-powered H.P.R. 3 Herald.

34 Avro York

The Avro 685 York came into being as a military transport for the RAF, evolved as a private venture to meet the requirements of Air Ministry Specification C.1/42 and flown for the first time (LV626) at Ringway on 5 July 1942. The York's design relied heavily on that of the Lancaster, utilising the bomber's wing, power units and dual tail assembly allied to a square-section fuselage of about twice the Lancaster's volume. Mounting the wing high while retaining Lancaster-length main-wheel legs ensured that the fuselage was suitably close to ground level to facilitate the loading of cargo, but the additional side area of the transport body necessitated the introduction of a central fin on the third and all subsequent aircraft. Although designed quickly, the York's production priority was low, and comparatively few were built until 1945, when a full-scale programme got under way. Up to April 1948, when production ended, two hundred and fifty-six Yorks were built, most of them for RAF Transport Command. The first civil Yorks were five RAF aircraft allocated to BOAC in 1944 as 12-seat passenger/cargo aircraft, with which the airline inaugurated a service to Cairo in April. BOAC operated (though not all at one time) a total of forty-three Yorks, including four reserved for crew training. This total included nineteen acquired from its sister airline BSAA after the dissolution of that airline in 1949. Most of these had a standard 18-seat day-time interior, although a few 12-berth sleeper models were also in use. Overseas operators included South African Airways and FAMA of Argentina. Another pioneer operator of Yorks was the British independent Skyways, which had had three of the early Yorks in 1945–46; and when BOAC began to sell off its Yorks in 1951, Skyways built up a substantial fleet of these aircraft. When Hastings transports began to replace the RAF Yorks from 1951 (although the last York was not retired from service until five years later), about thirty more Yorks came on to the British civil register during the early 1950s. At the end of 1957, BOAC disposed of its last two Yorks to Skyways, and for the next few years Skyways, Dan-Air and Hunting Clan were the principal operators. About a score of Yorks remained in service in the United Kingdom in 1960, but within the next two or three years these had all been withdrawn. A surviving airworthy example in Britain is G-AGNV, preserved by the Skyfame Museum at Staverton, Gloucestershire. The first aircraft, LV626, was re-engined with Bristol Hercules radials as the prototype for a York II, but no production of this model was undertaken.

35 Lockheed Constellation

One of the veterans of trans-Atlantic and other long-haul air routes since 1945, the Constellation and its descendants have performed yeoman service for two decades, and about twenty were still in airline service in 1970. The Constellation's design originated in 1939 as a 40-passenger aircraft to the requirements of TWA (who ordered forty) and, later, Pan American Airways, but the United States had entered World War 2 by the time the first prototype (NX25600) was flown on 9 January 1943, and the Constellation's first career was as a military transport under the designation C-69. A large C-69 order was later cut drastically, and by VJ-day fifteen of these had been accepted by the USAAF. The remainder were immediately converted to civilian interiors and allocated to commercial customers. As the L-049 Constellation, this early version received CAA operating approval on 11 December 1945. The L-049 was basically a 43/48-seat aircraft, with a high-density capacity for up to 60 passengers. The first two customers, as before, were Pan American and TWA. The former became the first airline to operate Constellations when it introduced the type on its New York–Bermuda route in February 1946; TWA, which received its first Constellation in November 1945, opened the first US–Europe service (to Paris) on 6 February 1946. On 1 July 1946 the first of five L-049's for BOAC (G-AHEJ *Bristol II*) opened a trans-Atlantic service between London and New York. The first wholly civil Constellation was the so-called 'gold plate' Model L-649. This was flown for the first time (NX101A) on 19 October 1946 and entered service (with Eastern Air Lines) in May 1947. With 2,500 hp R-3350-C18-BD1 engines, the L-649 was able to accommodate 48–64 passengers (maximum 81) or a maximum payload of 20,276 lb (10,197 kg). This version was itself replaced in production in 1947 by the L-749, to which standard a number of L-649's were later converted. The L-749 Constellation was basically similar to the L-649, with the same seating capacity, but having additional fuel storage within the wings, enabling non-stop flights to be made between New York and Paris (3,660 miles = 5,890 km). PanAm's NC86530 *Clipper America* started the first round-the-world air service in June 1947. The L-749A was a variant with sturdier landing gear, permitting the gross take-off weight to be increased by 5,000 lb (2,268 kg) to 107,000 lb (48,534 kg). Excluding twelve military L-749A's, total Constellation production of all variants reached two hundred and twenty-one (twenty-two C-69/L-049 conversions, sixty-six L-049's, twenty L-649/649A's and one hundred and thirteen L-749/749A's) before giving way to the Super Constellation in 1951.

36 Lockheed Super Constellation

Representing the greatest single stretch carried out on any propeller-driven airliner, the transformation of the already-long Constellation into the serpentine form of the Super Constellation took place in 1950. The insertion of additional sections fore and aft of the wing to lengthen the fuselage by 18 ft 4 in (5.59 m) was only one of several major design changes; others included a general reinforcing of the entire airframe, the provision of larger, rectangular passenger windows and a substantial increase in fuel capacity; and the utilisation of Wright R-3350 piston engines of greater power. To test all these modifications in the air the original Constellation (NX25600, re-registered NX6700) was turned into the prototype L-1049 Super Constellation, making its maiden flight in this form on 13 October 1950. The new 'Connie' proved to have excellent operating characteristics, but with 2,700 hp R-3350-CB1 engines was somewhat underpowered. Consequently only twenty-four L-1049's were built, for Eastern and TWA, the former airline leading in putting the type into service on 17 December 1951. The L-1049A and L-1049B were, respectively, the military RC-121D/WV-2 and -3 and the RC-121C/R7V-1, and from the latter was derived the next civil model, the L-1049C. Both the B and C models overcame the power shortage by using the Turbo Compound version of the R-3350 engine, which offered 3,250 hp for take-off, and successively later marks of the engine were selected for all subsequent Super Constellations. The first L-1049C (PH-TFP) was flown on 17 February 1953, and this type was first delivered to KLM and TWA, who commenced operating it in August and September 1953 respectively. Sixty of this version were completed, four of them as L-1049D cargo counterparts of the C model; the first D conversion flew in September 1954. Further detail refinements

appeared in the L-1049E, but only eighteen of these were completed; the remainder of the fifty-six originally ordered were completed during assembly, at their purchaser's request, as L-1049G's. (The L-1049F was a military model.) The L-1049G, known colloquially as the Super G, represented an even greater improvement than its predecessors, having 3,400 hp Turbo Compounds available optionally, more fuel (in wingtip tanks) and even better payload/range capabilities. The first Super G was flown on 12 December 1954, and entered service with Northwest Airlines in the spring of 1955; in addition to the thirty-eight former L-1049E's, sixty-six Super Constellations were completed as Super G's, and fifty-three more as cargo/passenger L-1049H's, bringing total civil production of the Super Constellation variants to two hundred and fifty-four aircraft. Maximum capacity of the two last-named versions was 95 passengers (L-1049G) or 24,293 lb (11,021 kg) of cargo (L-1049H). One further and final stretch of this highly elastic design produced the L-1649A Starliner, which flew for the first time on 11 October 1956. The Starliner was 2 ft 7 in (0·79 m) longer than the Super Constellation, seating 58–75 passengers normally, and was evolved to TWA's request as a counter to Douglas's long range DC-7C. An entirely new thin-section, straight-tapered wing, spanning 150 ft 0 in (45·72 m) and carrying much more fuel, did indeed give the Starliner more range than the DC-7C, but it was behind its rival in entering service (June 1957) and its career was overtaken by the big jets a year or two later. Forty-three Starliners were built, these going initially to TWA, Air France and Lufthansa. By 1970 only about forty members of the Super Constellation/Starliner family remained in regular airline service.

37 & 38 **Vickers Viscount**

The Brabazon Committee's Type IIB requirement, later covered by Ministry of Supply Specification 8/46, was for a 24-seat short/medium-range airliner for European routes, powered by four turboprop engines. Vickers, who had already made several design studies along similar lines, liaised with BEA in developing the proposed VC2 to meet this requirement, and were eventually rewarded by an order for two Type 609 prototypes. Construction of these began in December 1946, modified to a 32-seat capacity at the request of BEA, powered by Dart RDa. 1 engines, renumbered Type 630 and named Viceroy. The name was changed to Viscount in 1947 for diplomatic reasons after the partition of India. The first 630, G-AHRF, was flown at Wisley on 16 July 1948, but before the year was out BEA had been instructed to cancel its order, and the second prototype became a testbed for the Tay turbojet. However, with the higher-powered RDa. 3 available, Vickers embarked upon an enlarged, 53-seat development which reawakened BEA interest, and work on this continued under

Specification 21/49 as the Viscount 700. The prototype, G-AMAV, flew for the first time on 28 August 1950. A few days before this, BEA had completed nearly four weeks' intensive use of the 630 prototype, which it had borrowed to augment summer peak services. The passengers' reaction to the Viscount's speed, comfort and quietness, together with the airline's appreciation of its operating economy and ability, affirmed BEA's interest in the larger model, and an order for twenty-six Viscount 701's was placed before the end of the year. By the time the first of these entered service in April 1953, substantial orders for Viscount 700 variants had been placed by Air France, Aer Lingus, TAA and TCA. The last named order, received in November 1952, was the Viscount's first breakthrough into the lucrative North American market, and was soon followed by others from a number of US operators for the only propeller-turbine-powered airliner then in production anywhere in the world. The largest US orders, totalling more than sixty, came from Capital Airlines, but when this operator went bankrupt its Viscount fleet was taken over by United Air Lines; and United, together with TCA (now Air Canada), became the largest operators of Series 700 Viscounts. Although there are many Viscount Type numbers, signifying interior layouts to individual customer requirements, there are basically only three models in the 700 Series: the original 700, with Dart 505 or 506 engines; the 700D with

Dart 510's and extra fuel tankage; and the 770D, the North American equivalent of the 700D. Some Viscount 700D's were fitted with slipper fuel tanks on the wing leading edges. Excluding prototypes, two hundred and eighty-seven Series 700 Viscounts were built; about a hundred and forty were still in service early in 1970, a small number as military or business executive transports.

The promise of progressively more powerful versions of the Dart turbo-prop led Vickers in the early 1950s to propose a stretched version of the Viscount 700 with high-density seating for up to 86 passengers over shorter stage lengths. To do this it was proposed to extend the fuselage by as much as 13 ft 3 in (4·04 m) but, after ordering twelve Type 801's to this specification in February 1953, BEA asked instead for a 65-seat aircraft. This emerged as the Type 802, being only 3 ft 10 in (1·17 m) longer than the 700 and having Dart 510 engines. The Viscount 802 was first flown on 27 July 1956, and was put into BEA service in February 1957. Generally similar Series 800 Viscounts were completed for Aer Lingus, KLM, New Zealand National Airways and other customers, together with a batch of Dart 520-powered Type 806's for BEA, but the next major stage of development was the Series 810 with 1,990 ehp Dart 525's, flown for the first time (G-AOYU) on 23 December 1957. The Series 810, evolved initially to the requirement of Continental Airlines, was sub-sequently built in considerable numbers for Cubana, Lufthansa, Pakistan International, South African Airways, TAP and VASP. The 810's gross weight of 67,500 lb (30,618 kg) and 402 mph (647 km/hr) speed, compared to the 43,000 lb (19,504 kg) and 300 mph (483 km/hr) of the little Viscount 630 prototype, give some idea of the Viscount's development over the years. Seating has risen in proportion from the original 32 to the maximum of 70 which can be carried by some Viscount 810's. Viscount production on any scale ceased in 1959, though a few additional orders were executed between 1959 and 1964. Sixty-seven Series 800 and eighty-four Series 810 aircraft were completed, and the grand total of all Viscounts built amounted to four hundred and forty-four. Just over one hundred Series 800/810 aircraft were still commercially active at the beginning of 1970; these can be distinguished from the 700 Series by the longer fuselage and additional passenger windows forward of the wing, and by rectangular instead of oval doors.

39 Breguet Provence

An aeroplane whose shape and bulk made it easily recognisable, the Provence design originated in 1944, although the prototype (F-WFAM), known as the Br 761 Deux Ponts and powered by four 1,580 hp SNECMA-built Gnome-Rhône 14R radial engines, did not fly until 15 February 1949. It was followed by a pre-production batch of three

Br 761S's in which these were replaced by 2,020 hp Pratt & Whitney R-2800-B31 engines. All four aircraft were intended for a four-man flight crew and, apart from the powerplant, modified wingtips and the addition of a third, central fin, the Br 761S's were similar to the prototype.

One of the pre-series machines was leased for a time to Air Algérie, and one later operated in Silver City colours before, in the middle 1950s, all three were handed over to the Armée de l'Air for service trials. Meanwhile, in 1951 Air France had ordered twelve examples of a developed version, the Br 763. Equipped with more powerful R-2800 engines, the Br 763 also had strengthened wings of greater span and a cabin redesigned for a three-man crew; it made its maiden flight on 20 July 1951. The first Br 763 was delivered to Air France in August 1952, and under the class name Provence the type was first put into regular service, Lyons–Algiers, on 16 March 1953. Six of these aircraft were handed over to the Armée de l'Air in 1964 for military duties in the Far East, but Air France continued to operate the type, with the name Universel, in a freighter role until 1971. The Br 763, which has been described as 'a glutton for work', has a double-deck interior layout which in the passenger configuration originally seated 59 on the upper deck and 48 on the lower; 135 people could be carried in a high-density layout. As an all-cargo aeroplane it could accommodate some 11 tons of freight; it could

also be operated as a mixed passenger/cargo aircraft or vehicle ferry. In the mid-1960s the Br 763 was flown on trans-Mediterranean routes to Corsica and North Africa, where it provided valuable supply support to companies developing the petroleum and mineral resources of the Sahara desert. The six former Air France Provences, under the military name Sahara, were allocated to the 64e Escadre de Transport along with four Br 765's with removable cargo doors and the original trio of Br 761S's.

40 Aviation Traders Carvair

The need for an aeroplane such as the Carvair arose in the late 1950s when Air Charter Ltd of Southend, an associate of Aviation Traders (Engineering) Ltd, began to seek a replacement for its ageing Bristol Freighters. What they wanted was a four-engined aeroplane, capable of flying five cars and 25 passengers over fairly long ranges, which would be comparatively cheap both to buy and to operate. No existing design filled the bill, and the cost of an entirely new design would have been prohibitive. Aviation Traders met the challenge by producing an adaptation of the Douglas DC-4, thus combining the advantages of using an already proven airframe with low initial cost. With technical assistance from Douglas, Aviation Traders began to convert their first machine, the alterations consisting basically of substituting an entirely new and longer front fuselage, with a sideways-hinged nose door through which the vehicles could be loaded, and an enlarged DC-7C pattern vertical tail. The flight deck was situated high above the front cargo hold. The aeroplane was named Carvair – a contraction of 'car-via-air' – and the first converted machine, G-ANYB, made its maiden flight at Southend on 21 June 1961. It had already flown 37,000 hours as a DC-4. In March 1962 the Carvair went into service with the Channel Air Bridge division of Air Charter (by then incorporated in British United Air Ferries), on vehicle ferry routes to the Continent. The Carvair's main freight hold is 68 ft (20·73 m) long, holding four large or five standard size cars; the rear passenger cabin, 12 ft 2 in (3·71 m) long, seats 23 passengers, and, with the 151 cu ft (4·27 m³) under-floor baggage hold, gives a total internal volume of 4,630 cu ft (131·1 m³). Alternative passenger and/or freight accommodation can be installed, a maximum passenger load of 85 being possible. British United Air Ferries operated a fleet of ten Carvairs on both long- and short-haul routes; the three flown by Aer Lingus were equipped to carry racehorses as well as vehicles and other cargo; Aviaco used three Carvairs on mixed-traffic runs from Spain to France and the Balearic Islands; Compagnie Air Transport operated the two freighters formerly belonging to Interocean Airways of Luxembourg, and converted to a 55-passenger layout; and Ansett/ANA operated three Carvairs, two of them as pure freighters with slightly enlarged nose doors.

41 Bristol Britannia

The Britannia, or Bristol Type 175, was one of several designs submitted in response to a 1947 specification to fulfil the future requirements of BOAC. From these the airline selected a relatively small (48-seat) aircraft with Centaurus piston engines, and in July 1948 three prototypes were ordered on its behalf by the Ministry of Supply. Four months later BOAC indicated that it would have twenty-five of these aircraft. The first six only would have Centaurus engines, the remainder the Bristol Proteus turbo-prop, which all along had been nominated as an alternative power-plant; and the aircraft would be increased in size to seat up to 74 people. In the event only two proto-types (Britannia 101) were completed; the first of these (G-ALBO) flew on 16 August 1952 with Proteus 625's, the second, G-ALRX, with Proteus 705's. Production ensued of fifteen Britannia 102's for BOAC which, after some development delays, entered service on the Corporation's South African routes on 1 February 1957 and to Australia a month later. BOAC had reserved the final ten of its order for an enlarged version capable of working the North Atlantic route non-stop with a more worthwhile payload. The first appeared in the form of the Britannia 300, in which 4,120 ehp Proteus 755 engines were combined with a 10 ft 3 in (3·12 m) longer fuselage, seating up to 133 tourist-class passengers. The proto-type for this series was the Britannia 301 (G-ANCA), which made its first flight on 31 July 1956. It was succeeded by seven production aircraft with increased tankage, laid down as Britannia 302's for BOAC, whose order had meanwhile been reduced to that figure. In the event, however, BOAC relinquished its claim to these aircraft, which were completed and delivered as Britannia 302's (two for Aeronaves de Mexico), 305's (two for Transcontinental SA), 307's (two for Air Charter) and one 309 (for Ghana Airways). The last five were to have gone to Northeast Airlines, but the American company found itself unable to finance them. The principal long-range model was the Series 310. Its prototype, the Britannia 311 (G-AOVA), flew on 31 December 1956, later being converted to a 312 for BOAC but then diverted to replace the crashed G-ANCA as a development aircraft. BOAC ordered ten Britannia 312's in August 1955, later increasing this to eighteen. Delivery began in September 1957; trans-Atlantic services started on 19 December. Britannias (100 and 310 Series) were operated by many of BOAC's overseas associate airlines. Trans-Atlantic services were also flown by the Israeli airline El Al (Britannia 313's) and Canadian Pacific (314's); other customers including Hunting Clan (two 317's) and Cubana (four 318's). Three Britannia 252's and twenty 253's, basically similar to the Series 310 except for a large forward freight door, were completed by Short Bros for RAF Transport Command as Britannia C. Mk 1's. The final stage in the Britannia's development was the Series 320:

this differed chiefly in having 4,445 ehp Proteus 765 engines. The only Britannias actually designated in this series were two 324's for Canadian Pacific, but one Britannia 312, one 313 and two 318's were also completed to similar standard, and other Series 310 aircraft were re-engined with Proteus 765's. BOAC retired its long-range fleet in 1965, many of these going to British Eagle. Some forty Britannias remained in service in 1970, mostly of the 310 series and nearly all of them in the fleets of European operators.

42 Canadair CL-44 Forty-Four

In spite of a strong superficial resemblance to the Bristol Britannia, from which it was derived, the Canadair Forty-Four is an almost complete redesign of the British airliner. The first step leading to the ultimate production of the commercial CL-44 was taken in 1956, when Canadair began studies to evolve a trooper/freighter transport for the Royal Canadian Air Force. The Argus maritime patrol aircraft, then in production, had been based on the Britannia, and to take the same aircraft as a basis for developing the transport requirement was a logical extension of the company's licence arrangement with Bristol. The RCAF's need was fulfilled in the form of the CL-44-6, twelve of which were delivered from 1960 as the CC-106 Yukon. These aircraft had conventional side-loading facilities via front and rear fuselage doors, but in aiming for the civil market Canadair had decided, in November 1958, to pursue the novel idea of swinging the entire tail section of the aeroplane to one side to enable straight-in loading of bulky cargoes. The first machine with this feature, designated CL-44D4 and registered CF-MKP-X, was flown for the first time on 16 November 1960. First customer was The Flying Tiger Line, which received the first of an order for twelve CL-44D4's in May 1961. The first of seven for Seaboard World Airlines was delivered in June – in which month the aircraft also received its FAA certification – and both airlines commenced operations with the freighter in July. Seaboard leased one of its Forty-Fours to BOAC from 1963–65 for trans-Atlantic cargo services. Slick Airways received the first of four CL-44D4's in January 1962; the fourth customer was Loftleidir of Iceland, whose three brought total production of the D4 model to twenty-seven. Loftleidir operated its Forty-Fours as 160-seat low-fare passenger aircraft across the North Atlantic, adding to its fleet in 1966 a fourth aircraft completed as a CL-44J. This is a stretched version, also known as the Canadair 400, with a 15 ft 1¾ in (4·62 m) longer fuselage, seating up to 214 passengers, though still retaining the swing-tail arrangement of the D4. It flew for the first time (as CF-SEE-X) on 8 November 1965. Loftleidir's three original CL-44D4's were later converted to 44J standard.

43 Lockheed Electra

Lockheed's first appraisals of the short/medium-range airliner market were made in the early 1950s,

experience with building the C-130 Hercules military transport leading it to choose a turboprop rather than a pure-jet design. In 1954 it offered to American Airlines a high-wing project, the CL-303, with four Dart or Eland engines, but this proved too small for American's needs, as did the low-wing, Allison-powered CL-310 which was Lockheed's next proposal. However, in January 1955 American issued its detailed requirements to the US industry at large, to which Lockheed announced in June a scaled-up development of the CL-310 known as the L-188 Electra. American's order for thirty-five Electras 'off the drawing board' was quickly followed by one from Eastern Air Lines for forty. A year after its announcement the Electra had attracted orders for a hundred and twenty-eight aircraft, and this total had risen to a hundred and forty-four by the time the first prototype (N1881) was flown on 6 December 1957. A second prototype was flown on 13 February 1958 and a third (N1883) on 19 August 1958, the latter being used as the US Navy's aerodynamic prototype for the P-3 (then P3V-1) Orion anti-submarine aircraft. On 22 August FAA type certification was granted (at a gross weight of 113,000 lb (51,257 kg)) to the L-188A, the initial production version. The first L-188A (N5501) was delivered to Eastern and put into scheduled operation on 12 January 1959; American Airlines' first Electra entered service eleven days later. The L-188A was supplanted as the standard model by the L-188C, which has increased fuel capacity and gross weight and seats up to 99 passengers. The first recipient of the L-188C was Northwest Airlines. The only European operator to order the Electra was KLM Royal Dutch Airlines, whose first L-188C was delivered (as PH-LLA *Mercurius*) in the autumn of 1959, entering service in December. A setback to the Electra's career occurred after serious accidents to a Braniff aircraft in September 1959 and one of Northwest's aircraft in the following March. Speed restrictions were imposed (until January 1961) while all Electras on the production line and in service underwent a strengthening of the nacelle and surrounding wing structure. A total of one hundred and seventy Electras – the first US-designed and built propeller-turbine airliner – were built.

44   Vickers Vanguard

Although, in 1951, British European Airways still had nearly two years to wait before receiving its first Viscounts, the airline was already looking ahead to the time when it would need to replace them, and over the next few years a considerable number of design studies were considered in conjunction with Vickers. Some, naturally enough, were based on Viscount components, but in 1953 the Type 900 was begun as an entirely new and independent design. The BEA specification called for Rolls-Royce Tyne engines, a capacity of 93 passengers or a 21,000 lb (9,525 kg) payload and a gross weight of 115,000 lb (52,163 kg), but further examination re-

vealed that the payload/range performance of such an aeroplane would not be acceptable economically. Vickers therefore scaled up the design to 135,000 lb (61,235 kg) as the Type 950. Work on building the 950 prototype, G-AOYW, began and in July 1956 BEA placed an order for twenty production Type 951's. Six months later came a second order for twenty, later increased to twenty-three, from Trans-Canada Air Lines. The Canadian machines, designated Type 952, were to have Tyne RTy.11 Mk 512 engines of 5,545 ehp and a 146,500 lb (66,450 kg) gross weight, and in the summer of 1958 BEA also decided to take advantage of the heavier version. Accordingly it reduced its Vanguard 951 order to six, making up the total with fourteen 953's having the same gross weight as the Canadian model but retaining the Tyne 506 power-plant of the 951. The maiden flight of G-AOYW took place on 20 January 1959, to be followed on 22 April by G-APEA, the first of the 951's for BEA. Some non-scheduled BEA Vanguard flights began in December 1960, and on 1 March 1961 the airline began scheduled services. TCA Vanguard services began a month earlier, and in May 1961 the Vanguard 953 entered BEA service. At the beginning of 1971 TCA (now Air Canada) still had eight Vanguards in its fleet; all nineteen of the BEA aircraft were still retained on charge, and were in the process of transformation into Merchantman freighters. All accommodation (up to 139 passengers can be carried, according to layout) is on the upper deck of the 'double-bubble' fuselage.

45 Ilyushin Il-18 Moskva ('Coot')

It is no coincidence that one of the most elegant Soviet transport designs of recent years has also been the country's most exportable product. The Ilyushin bureau began work on the Il-18 design in 1955, following discussions with Aeroflot for a 75-seat turboprop aircraft for trunk and principal feeder services. The prototype (CCCP-L5811) was flown for the first time by veteran test pilot Vladimir Kokkinaki in July 1957, making its public début at Moscow's Vnukovo airport later that month. Three further trials aircraft were followed by an initial batch of twenty Il-18's. Ten of these were powered, like the prototype, with 4,000 ehp Kuznetsov NK-4 engines, while the remaining ten, for comparative purposes, were fitted with Ivchenko AI-20's of similar output. The latter engine was subsequently standardised for all further production Il-18's. An exhaustive two-year proving programme, during which the aircraft established a number of records, was conducted before the first Aeroflot passenger services with Il-18's were inaugurated on 20 April 1959. Further records and worldwide demonstration flights were made later that year, and from 1960 onwards several non-Soviet airlines began to operate the type. In 1971 these included Air Guinée (three), Air Mali (three), Balkan Bulgarian (twelve), CAAC (seven), CSA (eleven), Cubana

(five), Interflug (twelve), LOT (eight), Malév (nine), Tarom (fourteen) and UAA (five). The standard Il-18V has normal seating for 90 passengers, or 110 in a high-density layout. Other variants include the 122-seat Il-18E, which has 4,250 ehp AI-20M engines replacing the AI-20K's of other models; and the basically similar Il-18D, with substantially greater fuel capacity. All versions carry a normal flight crew of five, and the internal standards of accommodation and comfort are well up to the best comparable western types. By the end of 1971 total Il-18 production had reached more than seven hundred aircraft, the major share of these being in Aeroflot or foreign military service.

46 Antonov An-10A Ukraina ('Cat') and An-12 ('Cub')

The An-10 design was evolved to meet domestic civil and military requirements for a large passenger and freight-carrying aircraft for use from second-class airfields and those with unprepared landing strips. The design was begun in November 1955, following the general pattern of the smaller, twin-engined An-8. The high wing position conferred a double advantage, facilitating cargo loading arrangements and keeping the propellers well above ground level, thus reducing the risk of damage on rough airstrips. The first An-10 made its maiden flight at Kiev in March 1957 under the command of Y. I. Vernikov, and bore the fictitious registration CCCP-L1957. An initial batch of twenty aircraft was built, ten

138

powered by Kuznetsov NK-4 turbo-props and the remaining ten by Ivchenko AI-20 engines; the latter was subsequently adopted as standard powerplant. Initial stability problems were overcome by applying marked anhedral to the outer wing sections, and adding lozenge-shaped endplate auxiliary fins to the tailplane and an elongated fin beneath the tail cone. In this form the An-10 entered Aeroflot passenger service from Simferopol to Moscow and Kiev on 22 July 1959. Passenger accommodation was increased to 84 from the original 75 planned, and a prolonged route-proving programme of freight-carrying to Siberia was begun. However, a comparatively small number of An-10's (possibly no more than the original twenty) was completed before they were replaced on the production line by an improved model, the An-10A. This, which has become the major production model, is a 100-seater with twin under-tail strakes but minus the auxiliary finlets of the An-10; and it has a 6 ft 7 in (2·00 m) longer fuselage. The An-10A entered Aeroflot passenger service in February 1960, and in the following year was also employed (with a ski landing gear) to carry supplies to Soviet polar bases. Other events in 1961 included a closed-circuit speed record for propeller-driven aircraft of 454 mph (731 km/hr). The An-10A, which carries a flight crew of five, can seat up to 130 people in a high-density layout.

The An-12 is basically a freighter counterpart to the An-10A Ukraina. The principal differences between the two can be seen in the rear fuselage shape, which in the An-12 is swept upwards to a much-modified vertical tail and incorporates a rear-loading door which can be lowered to act as a ramp for the loading of vehicles and other large cargo. The military troop- or freight-carrier serves in some numbers with several Middle Eastern, African and Asian states as well as the Soviet Air Force. Others are in service with Aeroflot for general cargo-carrying duties, including the transportation of agricultural and industrial machinery; one (CCCP-11359) has been used to transport scenery and other equipment to various European centres for the Bolshoi Ballet Company, and the aircraft has been extensively tested and used by the Russians in Arctic and Antarctic areas. Aeroflot also introduced on its Moscow–Paris service in February 1966 a mixed passenger/cargo version in which 14 passengers are accommodated in a pressurised compartment ahead of the cargo hold. Civil An-12's have also appeared in the colours of Bulair, Cubana, Ghana Airways and LOT. In the civil version a smooth fairing replaces the tail gun position of the military model.

47 Tupolev Tu-114 ('Cleat')

The Tu-114 *Rossiya* (Russia) prototype attracted as much attention at the 1959 Salon de l' Aéronautique as did the Antonov An-22 six years later, for it was at that time the world's largest commercial passenger aircraft. It is also the only swept-wing airliner with turboprop engines. As its general layout reveals, it is a sister design to the Tu-95 bomber developed for the Soviet Air Force, and employs basically the same wing, engine and landing-gear units and a similar tail assembly. Whereas the Tu-95 is a mid-wing aeroplane, however, the Tu-114 employs a low wing position combined with an entirely new and much larger fuselage seating a maximum (over short ranges) of 220 passengers and incorporating a 48-seat restaurant cabin amidships. Development and construction of this turboprop airliner took place at a time when the world's airlines were engaged on a spending spree for pure-jet types, and it is a mark of the capabilities of its Kuznetsov engines that the Tu-114's top cruising speed was little less than that of such contemporaries as the Caravelle and Comet 4 – not to mention the prodigious payloads and ranges of which the Russian aeroplane was capable. These latter attributes are borne out by over thirty speed and height records, with various payloads, set up by the Tu-114 in 1960–61. First flight of the Tu-114 prototype was made by A. Yakimov at Vnukovo in October 1957, neatly timed to coincide with the 40th anniversary of the October Revolution. Following the various record attempts and the normal flight development programme, the Tu-114 finally entered service with Aeroflot on 24 April 1961 on the 4,350-mile (7,000-km) route from Moscow to Khabarovsk in eastern Siberia. Some two and a half years later the Tu-114 opened a non-stop

service to Cuba, bringing Havana within 20 hours flying time of the Russian capital. Normal Aeroflot seating is for 170, mostly tourist class. Its fleet of Tu-114's is believed to number between twenty and thirty: this includes a small number of the Tu-114D, a variant using a much slimmer fuselage – probably a direct adaptation of that of the Tu-95 – which is employed for very long-range transport of urgent mail or freight or small numbers of passengers. The prototype Tu-114D made news in the spring of 1958 by flying a non-stop round trip from Moscow to Irkutsk and back, a total of 5,280 miles (8,500 km), at an average speed of 497 mph (800 km/hr).

48 **De Havilland Comet 1 and 2**
The Brabazon Committee, formed during World War 2 to formulate post-war requirements for British civil aircraft, supported the notion of a pure-jet transport only as a modest-capacity aeroplane for medium distances. De Havilland, on the other hand, felt that the jet could hold its own, financially, with higher loads over longer stage lengths; and by 1945 had evolved a tail-less design powered by four DH Ghost turbojets. After consultation with BOAC, however, a more orthodox design was adopted, and two prototypes were ordered by the Ministry of Supply to Specification 22/46. The first of these (G-5-1, later G-ALVG) was flown on 27 July 1949, by which time the aeroplane had been developed into a 36-seater; and the second, G-

ALZK, on 27 July 1950. The latter made extensive route-proving flights in the colours of BOAC, who had nine Comet 1's on order, and on 9 January 1951 the first production model for the airline (G-ALYP) made its maiden flight powered by four 4,450 lb (2,018 kg) st Ghost 50 Mk 1's. In May and August 1952, Comet services were inaugurated to Johannesburg and Colombo – the first by jet airliner anywhere in the world; services to Singapore and Tokyo opened in October 1952 and April 1953. No further Comet 1's were built, the next model being the 44-seat Comet 1A with 5,000 lb (2,268 kg) st Ghost 50 Mk 2's and increased range at higher all-up weights. During 1952–53 ten Comet 1A's were delivered to Air France (three), Canadian Pacific (two), UAT (three) and No 412 Transport Squadron of the RCAF (two). Meanwhile, on 16 February 1952, a Comet 1 (G-ALYT), which had been set aside for flight development of the Rolls-Royce Avon, was flown with four 6,600 lb (2,994 kg) st Avon 502's; and, re-styled Comet 2X, became the prototype for the Comet 2. Although still basically a 44-seater, the Comet 2 had a 3 ft (0·91 m) longer fuselage, additional fuel and a higher gross weight. Its four 7,300 lb (3,311 kg) st Avon 503 engines were installed with the outward-curving jet pipes which are a feature of subsequent marks. The first production Comet 2 (G-AMXA) was flown on 27 August 1953, and twenty-two more were in varying stages of completion when, in April 1954, further work

was halted and all Comets in service grounded. This followed the accident on 8 April, the fifth since October 1952 involving Comets and the fourth to involve loss of lives. There followed the now-celebrated salvage act and exhaustive structural investigation which identified fatigue as the cause of these accidents; and fifteen of the Comet 2's were later completed in accordance with its recommendations. Ten went to No 216 Squadron and three to No 90 Group of the RAF; the other pair became Comet 2E's retained for further Avon engine development. The RCAF 1A's and two of those belonging to Air France were rebuilt as 1XB's to the revised standard with 5,500 lb (2,495 kg) st Ghost 50 Mk 4's; the former pair were restored to service in September 1957, the others being repurchased by the Ministry of Supply. During almost two years' service the Comet 1's and 1A's flew over thirty thousand revenue hours; what was lost through those tragic accidents – even though the aeroplane itself was completely vindicated – can never be calculated.

49 Tupolev Tu-104 ('Camel')

The existence of the Soviet Union's first jet airliner became known outside Russia when the prototype (CCCP-L5400) brought General Serov to London Airport on 22 March 1956. This machine had then been flying for about a year, being joined on 17 June 1955 by the first of a pre-production batch of Tu-104's built for evaluation. Appearing as it did during the temporary eclipse of the Comet and more than two years before the entry of the Boeing 707 into service, the Tu-104 would have attracted plenty of attention even if it had not been of Russian origin; but it attracted even more because it was clearly an adaptation of the Tu-16 'Badger' medium bomber, about which little was known in the west at that time. Its qualities as an airliner were denigrated by many simply because of its military origins, and uncomplimentary remarks were passed on its 'Victorian' cabin décor; but the choice of the Tu-104 to make that particular visit to Britain was clearly made on grounds of prestige, for the aeroplane had not at that time entered airline service in its homeland. Deliveries of production Tu-104's to Aeroflot began in May, and the first domestic jet service (Moscow–Irkutsk) was opened on 15 September 1956. The 50-seat Tu-104 was purely an interim model, for in 1956 work was already in hand to produce the 70-seat Tu-104A, which in the following autumn set many world speed-with-payload and height-with-payload records. By the end of 1957 the Tu-104A was in service with CSA, which eventually operated six; Aeroflot deliveries did not begin until 1958, but eventually increased until the Tu-104A was the most widely used model. Aeroflot was the only operator of the Tu-104B, a 100-seat development with a 3 ft 11½ in (1·21 m) longer fuselage, which appeared on Russian internal routes from 15 April 1959. In 1962 many Tu-104A's were modified internally to seat 100 passengers in the standard-length fuselage, these converted aircraft being designated Tu-104V. Generally speaking, the Tu-104 and Tu-104B are used on domestic services, production being of the order of fifty and one hundred respectively; while the hundred or more Tu-104A's are reserved for international routes. A high proportion of these were believed to be still in service in 1971, and their success is no doubt one reason why two other projected developments were not pursued. The first of these, appearing in 1957, was the Tu-110 with four Lyulka turbojet engines, the second being the Tu-104E, which appeared in 1960 and was powered by two RD-3M turbojets with increased-diameter intakes.

50 Tupolev Tu-124 ('Cookpot')

Despite an external resemblance to the Tu-104, from which it was obviously developed, the Tu-124 is a much smaller aeroplane and was intended primarily to replace the piston-engined Il-14 on short and medium stage routes in the Soviet Union and other Communist bloc countries. It also claims the distinction of being the Soviet Union's first turbofan-powered commercial type to go into regular operation, having flown its first scheduled service for Aeroflot (on the Moscow–Tallin route) on 2 October 1962 – some two years ahead of such western fanjets as the BAC One-Eleven. The prototype Tu-124 (CCCP-L45000), evolved under the designership of A. A. Archangelski, was flown in June 1960, and preliminary details of the aircraft were released by the USSR shortly afterwards. It is approximately three-quarters the size of the Tu-104, and can also be distinguished on the ground by its much shorter-stroke landing gear. A flight crew of three is normally carried, and the Tu-124 is in service with four basic interior layouts. The original Tu-124 had seating for 44 passengers, but the standard (and most widely used) model at present is the 56-seat Tu-124V. De luxe interiors are available in the Tu-124K for 36 people, and for 22 in the Tu-124K2, which are otherwise identical. The Tu-124 is now one of Aeroflot's most numerous types, and is complementary to the larger rear-engined Tu-134, providing high-speed inter-city travel in areas where the traffic growth is as yet insufficient to justify the use of the larger machine. The Czechoslovak airline CSA received three Tu-124's, one of which was the first example of this type to visit Britain in 1965; and East Germany's Interflug also operates the type. About a hundred are estimated to be in service with Aeroflot. Tu-124's have also been delivered to the East German Luftstreitkräfte and the Indian Air Force.

51 Boeing 737

It was something of a novelty for Boeing to be in the position of a late starter in the field of commercial jet transport, but the career of the Boeing 737 does not appear to have suffered unduly from coming late on the scene. Boeing's announcement of the 737 as its candidate in the short-haul jet market came on 22 February 1965, only three days before the maiden flight of one rival (the DC-9) and some six weeks before the other major contender (the BAC One-Eleven) entered airline service. It had already progressed from the original conception of a 60-seater to that of an aeroplane with accommodation for 75–103 passengers, and simultaneously with its disclosure Boeing was able to announce details of the first order, from Lufthansa, for twenty-one aircraft. The 737's external similarity to other Boeing airliners should not obscure the fact that it is essentially a new design; on the other hand, it has some 60 per cent commonality of structure and internal systems with its immediate predecessor, the Boeing 727. Furthermore, the retention of the same 12 ft 4 in (3·76 m) diameter fuselage as the earlier Boeings has contributed much to its roominess and appeal. Leading-edge Krueger flaps and triple-slotted trailing-edge flaps are combined with other wing high-lift devices to give the 737 a first-class small-airfield performance for a twin-jet machine. The first flight was made on 9 April 1967, and by 30 April 1971 total orders had reached two hundred and seventy-eight, most of which had been delivered. Lufthansa's order was for the basic 737 Series 100, which entered service on 10 February 1968, but the majority of subsequent orders have been for the 6 ft 4 in (1·93 m) longer Series 200. This seats up to 125, has larger doors and slightly modified tail surfaces, and flew for the first time on 18 August 1967. The second 737 customer, and first to order the Series 200, was United Air Lines, which had ordered seventy-five by 1970. The 737-200 is the 'local service' commuter airliner member of the family, whereas the smaller 737-100 will operate over stage lengths up to 1,400 miles (2,253 km). Alternative versions of the Model 737-200 include the mixed-traffic -200C; the 'quick-change' 737-200 QC, which can be converted from passenger to cargo interior – or vice versa – in less than half an hour; and the 737-200 Business Jet executive transport. In 1971 Boeing was introducing 'Advanced' versions of each 737-200 model, with improved short-field take-off and landing characteristics and, eventually, the option of 15,500 lb (7,030 kg) st JT8D-15 engines.

52 **Dassault Mercure**

Development of this high-capacity twin-turbofan transport was started in 1967, after Dassault had carried out extensive studies of the world airline market. The most significant fact to emerge from these studies was that there was no suitable aircraft tailored directly to the needs of short-haul operations – routes of up to 930 miles (1,500 km) in length. The shorter the stage length, the greater is the percentage of block time spent in climbing out of airports and descending into them; therefore, the less time that is spent at optimum cruising conditions, the higher are the relative operating costs compared with longer-range

travel. Yet the majority of aircraft currently employed on these short routes – notably the Caravelle, One-Eleven, DC-9, Boeing 727 and Boeing 737 – were basically medium-range types, in versions stretched to carry extra passengers in an attempt to mitigate this economic imbalance. For service during the 1970s a new generation of 'airbus' types, such as the DC-10, TriStar and A 300B, were under development, but there seemed to be a gap in the market for a short-range 'mini-airbus' seating about 130–150 passengers. It is to fill this gap that the Mercure was evolved. Although designed by Dassault, the Mercure's production is a collaborative international venture, with Aeritalia (Fiat) contributing the tail assembly and tail-cone, CASA of Spain the entire front fuselage forward of the wing leading edge, and SABCA of Belgium the wing moving surfaces. Dassault is building the centre and rear fuselage, main wing structure and engine pylons. Since the selected powerplant, the Pratt & Whitney JT8D, is not notably one of the world's quietest engines, Dassault is working with SNECMA on a noise reduction system for installation on production aircraft. The six-abreast seating provides for up to 155 passengers, giving the Mercure a ratio of approximately one-third of a ton of take-off weight per passenger carried, compared with about half a ton per passenger on a typical medium-range airbus-type aircraft or one ton per passenger on a longer-range high-capacity aircraft.

Two prototypes and a structural

test airframe are included in the development programme. The first prototype was flown on 28 May 1971 and was registered F-WTCC, a 'contrived' identity in which the last three letters signify Transport Court-Courrier (short-range transport). This aircraft was powered by 15,000 lb (6,804 kg) st JT8D-11 engines, but the more powerful JT8D-15 will power the second prototype (due to fly in July 1972) and the production aircraft. Certification is anticipated by March 1973, with deliveries beginning immediately afterwards. The only customer announced up to mid-1971 was Air Inter, which has an option on twelve Mercures for delivery in 1973–74.

53 & 54 **Aérospatiale Caravelle**
The Caravelle was the outcome of a specification issued in November 1951 to which six major French aircraft constructors submitted design proposals. The SNCA du Sud-Est put forward two projects in June 1952, one a triple-Atar design and the other based on the use of two then-undeveloped by-pass engines; the former, known as the X-210, was finally chosen – but as a twin-jet, using the more powerful Rolls-Royce Avon in place of the Atar. In January 1953 the Secrétariat-Générale à l'Aviation Civile et Commerciale ordered two flying prototypes and two static-test airframes to be built, and the first prototype (F-WHHH) made its maiden flight on 27 May 1955. The second followed on 16 May 1956, both aircraft being powered by 10,000 lb (4,536 kg) thrust Avon RA. 26

engines. The Caravelle -01 continued the flight-testing and certification programme, while the -02 flew extensive demonstration tours of Europe and the Americas. French certification was granted on 2 April and FAA type approval on 8 April 1958. The first production aircraft was flown on 18 May 1958. The first Caravelle I's, with 10,500 lb (4,763 kg) st Avon RA. 29 Mk 522's, were delivered in April 1959 to Air France and SAS, the latter being the first to enter service, on 26 April. The Caravelle IA was similar except for Avon 526 engines, but in 1959 there appeared the Caravelle III, powered by 11,700 lb (5,307 kg) st Avon Mk 527 engines which offered a much improved performance with higher loads. Nineteen Caravelle I's and thirteen Caravelle IA's were built; all except one Caravelle I (which had been lost in service) were converted in 1960–61 to Caravelle III standard, and a further seventy-eight of the latter model were built. Two non-airline Caravelle III's were completed: one became the Caravelle VII prototype when fitted with General Electric CJ805-23C turbofans, and the other was the Series III prototype (F-WJAK), converted to serve as prototype for the Caravelle VI. Flown for the first time on 10 September 1960, this has 12,200 lb (5,535 kg) Avon 531 engines. A variant is the VI-R, which has Avon 533's with thrust reversers, enlarged flight deck windows and was first flown (F-WJAP) on 6 February 1961. The model without thrust reversers is known as the

VI-N. Production of these two models totalled fifty-three VI-N's and fifty-six VI-R's. The first operator of the Caravelle VI-N was Sabena, which received its first aircraft in January 1961; United, six months later, was first into service with the VI-R. The fan-engined Caravelle 10 R has JT8D-7 turbofans of 14,000 lb (6,350 kg) thrust, but is otherwise similar to the VI-R. It flew for the first time on 18 January 1965 and twenty were eventually built. A development is the 11 R, first flown on 21 April 1967, which is a mixed-traffic version also having JT8D-7 engines but with a 3 ft 0⅔ in (0·93 m) extension of the fuselage forward of the wing, incorporating a large freight door. Six examples of this version were built.

A further-stretched version is the Caravelle Super B, a considerably more redesigned, second-generation model, incorporating many aerodynamic and technical improvements. Among the modifications are a 3 ft 3½ in (1·00 m) longer fuselage than the standard Caravelle, with the maximum seating increased to 104; a 4 ft 7 in (1·40 m) wider tailplane, with a 'bullet' fairing at its intersection with the fin and rudder; double-slotted flaps with greater travel; and a leading-edge root extension to the wings. Additional internal tankage is an optional extra. The first production Super B was flown on 3 March 1964, and the first delivery made on 25 July 1964, to Finnair. Total production of the Caravelle Super B was twenty-two aircraft. What is probably the

ultimate stretch of the original design appeared in the Caravelle 12, which was flown for the first time on 29 October 1970. This incorporates the airframe improvements of the Super B with more powerful JT8D-9 turbofan engines of 14,500 lb (6,577 kg) st and fore and aft extensions of the fuselage which increase the overall length to 118 ft 10½ in (36·24 m). During 1971 the Caravelle 12 (the only version still in production) was cleared for operation at a maximum take-off weight of 127,868 lb (58,000 kg) – maximum seating capacity is 140 – and twelve were on order.

55 & 56 BAC One-Eleven
Praised by pilots and passengers alike, the BAC One-Eleven has gone a long way towards fulfilling its role of jet successor to the Viscount. Admittedly, it has yet to approach the Viscount's record in numbers built or length of service, but by mid-1971 it already had more than six years of service behind it and orders had passed the two hundred mark. Its origins go back to the P-107 (later H-107) design evolved in 1956 by Hunting Percival Ltd. This was first framed to use Bristol Orpheus turbojets, but in September 1958 was re-tailored to Bristol Siddeley BS 75 turbofans instead. The project then languished until Hunting's absorption into the newly formed British Aircraft Corporation in 1960, when the design was reappraised in conjunction with Vickers' own VC11. As the BAC-107, the design was fattened up and given a 'T' tail; and an enlarged

development of this was announced in May 1961 as the BAC One-Eleven. Advantages offered included Rolls-Royce Spey engines (then under development for the Trident) and maximum seating for 69 passengers. Simultaneously with the publication of preliminary details, BAC announced their first order for the type, from British United Airways, for ten aircraft with options on another five. With its second order, the One-Eleven broke into the US domestic market, Braniff International ordering six. Before the first One-Eleven had flown, seven operators – three of them in the United States – had ordered forty-five aircraft – all of the initial model, the Series 200. The prototype (G-ASHG) flew for the first time on 20 August 1963. The first One-Eleven services by BUA began on 9 April 1965, only three days after its British C of A was issued; and Braniff began services on 25 April 1965, nine days after the issue of FAA type approval. Also in service since 1966 are the Series 300, 400 and 500, which carry more fuel and have more powerful Spey engines. Apart from a fractionally longer engine pod, the Series 300 and 400 are physically similar to the Series 200, and are powered by 11,400 lb (5,171 kg) st Spey Mk 511 turbofans. The development aircraft for these Series, G-ASYD, flew for the first time on 13 July 1965. The biggest single operator of the BAC One-Eleven is American Airlines, with a fleet of thirty Series 400's which it first put into service on 6 March 1966. In 1967, G-ASYD

was further modified, making another 'first' flight on 30 June of that year as development aircraft for the Series 500, a stretched version with 12,550 lb (5,692 kg) st Spey Mk 512 DW engines, extended wingtips giving a 5 ft 0 in (1·52 m) increase in span, and a 13 ft 10 in (4·22 m) increase in overall length permitting maximum seating capacity to be increased from 89 to 119 passengers. The normal flight crew is two on all models. On 27 August 1970 the long-suffering G-ASYD made yet another 'first' flight, this time as development aircraft for the Series 475, which combines the standard-length fuselage of the Series 400 with the wings and powerplant of the Series 500 and a modified landing gear for use at airports with low-strength runways. By June 1971 two hundred and eight One-Elevens had been ordered, comprising fifty-six Srs 200, nine Srs 300, seventy Srs 400, four Srs 475 and sixty-nine Srs 500.

57 McDonnell Douglas DC-9

The first US twin-jet to employ tail-mounted engines, the DC-9 was conceived at a time when the BAC One-Eleven – its closest rival – was already under development; when airlines were still digesting the financial effects of buying big jets; and when the DC-8 modification programme was costing Douglas a considerable sum of money. The main hope of success for a short/medium-haul jetliner lay in the US domestic market, which showed little interest in Douglas's original Model 2000 project of 1959. In 1962

Douglas brought out the Model 2086, also using JTF10 turbofans. More interest was shown in this, but by April 1963, when Douglas decided to go ahead with what had now become the DC-9, there were still no firm orders. The size of the aeroplane had been progressively increased, and the JT8D chosen as the definitive powerplant; and Douglas had enlisted de Havilland Canada and a score of US equipment and component manufacturers to share the costs. In May 1963 came the first order, from Delta Air Lines, for fifteen aircraft with options on fifteen more. Bonanza, whose intended purchase of One-Elevens had been vetoed by the US government, ordered three DC-9's, and Douglas started building two prototypes in July. They were rolled out together in January 1965, the first making its maiden flight on 25 February. Delta opened its DC-9 services on 29 November 1965. The Series 10 has since been built in two basic versions, the Model 11 with JT8D-5 turbofans and the Model 15 with more powerful JT8D-1's. Both have seating for up to 90 passengers. A stretched version, with wing span increased to 93 ft 5 in (28·47 m) and an overall length of 119 ft 3½ in (36·37 m), seats up to 115 passengers and is designated Series 30. It has full-span leading-edge slats and double-slotted flaps, 14,000 lb (6,350 kg) st JT8D-7 turbofans, 98,000 lb (44,452 kg) gross weight and a 26,156 lb (11,864 kg) payload. By 1 August 1966 – when the first DC-9-30 was flown – total DC-9 sales had reached

three hundred and seventy-five, of which two hundred and seventy-five were of Series 30 aircraft. Ten examples were built for SAS of the Series 20, which has the short body of the Series 10, the long-span wings of the Series 30 and 14,500 lb (6,577 kg) JT8D-9 engines. The JT8D-9 is also the powerplant of the Series 40, which has a further fuselage stretch giving an overall length of 125 ft 7¼ in (38·28 m) and a maximum seating capacity of 125 passengers, and flew for the first time on 28 November 1967. This version also was built to an order from SAS, with whom it entered service on 12 March 1968.

In addition to the standard passenger-carrying models of the DC-9, freight (DC-9F), convertible (DC-9CF) and passenger/freight (DC-9RC) versions are available of all Series. By the end of 1970 total sales of the DC-9 were in excess of six hundred, and of this total some two-thirds were of the Series 30. A variant of the DC-9-30, known as the C-9A Nightingale, is in service as a flying hospital and ambulance aircraft with the 375th Aeromedical Wing of Military Airlift Command of the USAF.

58 VFW-Fokker VFW 614

Billed as the first of a new generation of 'door-to-door' transport aeroplanes, the VFW 614 is attractive, unorthodox, and may be classed in a similar bracket operationally to the Soviet Union's Yak-40 as a small-capacity, very-short-range feeder-liner capable of operating from semi-prepared airfields. Its development has progressed slowly – it was started in 1962 and did not reach the flight test stage until 1971 – but this was due very largely to successive attempts by VFW to find an ideal set of partners to join in the venture. Another factor contributing to the lengthy gestation period is that VFW, having established first the basic role and design of the aircraft, only then approached Rolls-Royce and SNECMA to develop a turbofan engine that would enable it to meet the performance required. Initial impressions are that the result was worth waiting for, for by mid-1971 the parent company had received options for twenty-six aircraft from Bavaria Fluggesellschaft (three), Cimber Air (three), Filipinas Orient Airways (two), General Air (two), the Spanish Ministry of Aviation (one), STA (two), Sterling Airways (five), TABA (two) and Yemen Airlines (three), plus three others from an unnamed customer. VFW-Fokker has estimated that the sale of about one hundred and seventy-five aircraft will enable it to break even. The unique feature of the VFW 614 is the mounting of the engines on pylons above the wings, an arrangement dictated to a large extent by the need to have a short and sturdy landing gear for roughfield operations. The over-wing position is claimed to have several other advantages, such as inhibiting the ingestion of stones or other debris into the air intakes, minimising distortion of the engine air inlet pressure, permitting an undivided flap system, and greater safety in the

event of an emergency landing or an engine fire. Other features which help to make the aircraft less dependent upon airfield support equipment include a passenger door with built-in stairs, and an APU for ground conditioning and engine starting. The VFW 614 can take off and land in 3,950 ft (1,200 m) or less, and can be operated either as a passenger-carrier or as a freighter with a maximum payload of 8,598 lb (3,900 kg). In the latter form it will accept vehicles or standard pallets. Seating ranges from 36 to 44 (40 is standard), but break-even operating costs are claimed with only half of the available seats filled. Under normal operating conditions it is claimed to be cost-effective over stage lengths of 100 miles (160 km) upwards.

The development programme involves three prototypes (G1 to G3) and two structural test airframes, construction of which began in August 1968; the VFW 614G1 (D-BABA) flew for the first time on 14 July 1971, and first deliveries are due to be made in early 1973. Manufacture is shared with Dutch, Belgian, British and other German factories: VFW-Fokker itself builds the front and centre fuselage, MBB the rear fuselage and tail, Fokker-VFW the wings and engine pylons, Fairey and SABCA the wing moving surfaces, and Dowty the landing gear.

59 Fokker-VFW Fellowship

Fokker's proposed successor to the highly-successful Friendship took some time in coming to fruition, a result of deliberate policy following Fokker's declared objective that it should achieve steady sales over a long-term period, rather than collect a greater number of orders during a shorter production life. If the F.28 accomplishes this it will emulate its turboprop predecessor, from which many structural and production features have been inherited. The first details of the Fellowship were announced in April 1962, although detail design studies for a short/medium-haul fanjet had been under way at Fokker for more than two years before this. In February 1964 the project received a promise of financial support from the Netherlands government, and that summer agreements were signed whereby three other European manufacturers now collaborate in the production of the aeroplane. Short Bros and Harland is thus responsible for the outer wings and landing gear doors, while Germany's MBB (HFB) and Fokker's German partner VFW-Fokker between them produce centre and rear fuselage sections, tail units and engine nacelles. Fokker-VFW builds front and centre fuselages and wing root fairings. The Fellowship Mk 1000, the initial production version, seats from 40 to 65; it was first flown in prototype form (PH-JHG) on 9 May 1967, and three aircraft had flown by the end of the year. Certification of the Fellowship Mk 1000 by the Dutch authorities was granted on 24 February 1969, and was followed by FAA type approval on 24 March and German certification on 30 March. The first order for the F.28 was placed in November 1965 by LTU of Dusseldorf, though the first commercial services were inaugurated, on 28 March 1969, by the Norwegian operator Braathens, which has ordered five. Other orders, up to mid-1971, were from MacRobertson-Miller (five), the Argentine government (one), Aviaction (three), the Colombian government (one), Fairchild Hiller Corporation (ten, for resale in North America), Iberia (three), LTU (five) and Martinair-Holland (one). A short-fuselage version of the Fellowship, seating 50 passengers and powered by 9,730 lb (4,414 kg) st Rolls-Royce Trent engines, was proposed in 1967 by the Fairchild Hiller Corporation under the designation F-228. This was later abandoned, but on 28 April 1971 Fokker-VFW flew PH-JHG as the prototype for its stretched F.28 Mk 2000, which is 97 ft 1¾ in (29·61 m) long overall and seats up to 79 passengers. This version was to be available for airline service in 1972.

60 Tupolev Tu-134 ('Crusty')

The basic design layout of the Tu-104, developed via the fan-engined Tu-124, was taken a stage further in the Tu-134 which, in its early stages, was provisionally known as the Tu-124A. Several major design changes, however – notably the placing of the Soloviev fan engines at the rear of the aeroplane – justified the allocation of an entirely new bureau number. Work on the Tu-134 project began under Leonid Selyakov in June 1962, the first flight taking place in December 1963 with what the Russians described as 'existing' engines – presumably D-20 turbofans of the type that power the Tu-124. Production Tu-134's are powered by the improved D-30. Five pre-production aircraft were built; production Tu-134's have minor external refinements including a smaller dorsal fin fairing and tailplane 'bullet'. The Tu-134 is Russia's second rear-engined civil aircraft, and operationally may be regarded as the Soviet counterpart to the BAC One-Eleven and the McDonnell Douglas DC-9. It entered service with Aeroflot on internal routes during 1966, and began international operation in September 1967 on the Moscow–Stockholm service. Foreign operators in 1971 included Aviogenex of Yugoslavia (three), Balkan Bulgarian Airlines (six), Interflug (seven), LOT (six) and Malév (six). The configuration offers greater wing area and efficiency than that of the Tu-124, and greater seating capacity, the normal passenger complement being 64 (16 first-class and 48 tourist), maximum 72, with a flight crew of three. The Tu-134 has a maximum range with minimal payload of 2,175 miles (3,500 km), but is intended mainly for stage lengths of 310–1,240 miles (500–2,000 km). A soft-field landing gear (i.e. the front wheels of the main bogies touch down first) gives a good small-field performance in and out of second-class airports and those with grass runways, when the occasion arises.

As with most modern airliners, a stretched version is also available.

This is known as the Tu-134A, which has a 6 ft 10¾ in (2·10 m) increase in overall length enabling up to 80 passengers to be accommodated in a lengthened cabin. It has more sophisticated avionics, an APU, and engine thrust reversers, but is otherwise generally similar to the standard Tu-134. It entered Aeroflot service in the autumn of 1970.

61 Hawker Siddeley Trident

De Havilland's absorption into the Hawker Siddeley Group cannot disguise the ancestry of the Comet's successor in the BEA fleet, the (originally D.H. 121) Trident. The Trident was the outcome of a BEA requirement, outlined in July 1956, for a medium-range 'second generation' jet. It was the third de Havilland design considered for the role, the four-Avon D.H. 119 and the joint BEA/BOAC D.H. 120 both being discarded in the project stage. The D.H. 121, in company with the Avro 740 and Bristol 200, was intended at the outset as a 80/100-passenger aircraft for stage lengths of up to 1,000 miles (1,610 km), having 'more than two' engines and a minimum cruising speed of 600 mph (966 km/hr). In February 1958, BEA announced that it had chosen the de Havilland design. Six months later, the airline was given Ministry approval to proceed with its order, but another twelve months elapsed before it signed a firm contract for twenty-four aircraft. In January 1958 de Havilland formed a consortium with Hunting Aircraft and Fairey Aviation, for which the name of The Aircraft Manufacturing Company (Airco) was revived. The BEA requirement had undergone some revision by 1959, resolving into a smaller 75/80-seater powered by Spey turbofans in place of the more powerful RB.141's previously selected. In 1960 de Havilland became a part of the Hawker Siddeley Group and work started on the first batch of aircraft, to which the name Trident had by then been given. The first Trident 1 for BEA (there was no separate prototype), registered G-ARPA, made its maiden flight on 9 January 1962. With a wing span of 89 ft 10 in (27·38 m) and three 9,850 lb (4,468 kg) st Spey 505-5 engines, the Trident 1 has a gross weight of 115,000 lb (52,163 kg) and seats up to 103 passengers. Following the receipt of its C of A on 18 February 1964, the Trident 1 commenced scheduled services on BEA's European routes on 1 April. In June 1965 a BEA Trident 1 made the first automatic landing during a passenger service. Fifteen examples were built of the Trident 1E, a developed version with 11,400 lb (5,170 kg) st Spey 511-5's, a 5 ft 2 in (1·57 m) longer wing with full-span slats replacing the former drooped leading edge, up to 115 seats (139 in the four aircraft built for Channel Airways and BKS) and an enhanced payload/range performance. The first Trident 1E was flown on 2 November 1964 and the first delivery (to Pakistan International Airways) was made on 1 March 1966. In August 1965 BEA transformed its original option for twelve more Tridents into a firm

order for fifteen of the 2E version, which has a further 3 ft (0·91 m) increase in span and 11,930 lb (5,412 kg) st Spey Mk 512-5W's. At a gross weight of 143,500 lb (65,090 kg), it can carry 97 passengers (or up to 149 in high-density seating) over longer ranges than the Trident 1 and 1E. Delivery to BEA began on 15 February 1968, following the first flight of a 2E (G-AVFA) on 27 July 1967. BEA, which refers to this version simply as the Trident Two, began services with the 2E on 18 April 1968. In addition to the fifteen for BEA, two other examples of the 2E were built for Cyprus Airways, these being delivered in September 1969 and May 1970.

Latest version to be announced is the Trident 3B, of which twenty-six have been ordered by BEA as the Trident Three. This represents a further stretch of the basic design, having increased flap and total wing area compared with the 2E (though the span is the same) and an increase of 16 ft 5 in (5·00 m) in overall length. This permits the maximum seating capacity to be increased to 179. Basic powerplant is similar to the 2E, but the Trident 3B has in addition a 5,250 lb (2,381 kg) st Rolls-Royce RB. 162 installed at the base of the vertical tail, to improve performance during take-off and climb-out. First flights by the Trident 3B were made on 11 December 1969 (without the boost engine) and 22 March 1970 (with the RB. 162 installed), and this version of the aircraft entered service with BEA in April 1971.

No other turbine-engined transport aircraft in history has achieved such a remarkable commercial success as Boeing's short/medium-haul triple-turbofan 727. Since 5 December 1960, when Boeing announced its decision to go ahead with the 727, eight hundred and seventy-three of these aircraft had been ordered by 30 April 1971, and nearly all of these had been delivered. They serve with more than fifty airlines in every part of the world. From mid-1956, a hundred and fifty different design studies were undertaken, and sixty-eight of them tunnel-tested, before Boeing settled on the final layout in September 1960, which involved three rear-mounted engines. The 727 design is noteworthy in two particular aspects. The first is the system of wing high-lift devices, which were thoroughly tested on the 'Dash Eighty' 707 prototype and which give the 727 outstanding take-off and landing characteristics; the second lies in the fact that, from the cabin floor upwards, its fuselage cross-section is identical with the 707 series, making possible a considerable degree of commonality in construction and interior systems and seating arrangements to speed production. The Boeing 727 was originally designed as an 88/119-seater, but the standard production 727-100 can seat a maximum of 131 passengers; a typical mixed-class layout seats 94 people. In June 1961 Boeing started cutting metal for the first aircraft, and this made its maiden flight at Renton on 9 February 1963. The 727 had been launched with the news of orders from United and Eastern, each for forty of the Series 100, and the first to be delivered was handed over to the former operator on 29 October 1963; Eastern was the first to put the 727 into scheduled service, on 1 Februrary 1964. Lufthansa was the first non-American customer, with an order (since increased) for twelve which it operates under the name 'Europa Jet'. Later versions of the 727-100 are the -100C cargo version announced in 1964, and the -100QC (= Quick Change), which is similar but very quickly convertible to passenger and/or cargo operation; both models are in service. In September 1966 construction began of the first 727-200, a 20 ft 0 in (6·10 m) longer model with a standard powerplant of 14,500 lb (6,577 kg) st JT8D-9 turbofans and seating up to 189 passengers. The first 727-200 was flown on 27 July 1967 and received FAA Type Approval in the following November. This version is available optionally with 15,000 lb (6,804 kg) st JT8D-11 or 15,500 lb (7,030 kg) st JT8D-15 turbofans. As with the Series 100, C and QC versions are also available of the 727-200. In 1971 Boeing introduced the Advanced 727, initially to meet orders from Ansett/ANA and Trans-Australia Airlines. This is basically a 727-200 with improved interior layout, additional fuel capacity and a maximum ramp weight of 191,000 lb (86,635 kg).

By the end of 1970 the Boeing 727 had become both the biggest-selling and fastest-selling jet transport in the world, having surpassed the Boeing 707/720 series in a shorter period of time.

63 Yakovlev Yak-40 ('Codling')

In years gone by the design bureau headed by the veteran Soviet designer Aleksandir Yakovlev has produced piston- and jet-engined fighters, strike and training aircraft, piston-engined transports and helicopters. The latest addition to this wide range of subjects was not only Yakovlev's first entry into the realm of turbine-engined commercial transports but was also the first fan-engined feeder-liner to go into service anywhere in the world. It was evolved as a modern replacement for the piston-engined Lisunov Li-2 (licence DC-3), Il-14 and similar types on Aeroflot internal routes, and has been especially tailored for use from semi-prepared or grass airfields. As such it makes an interesting comparison with the German VFW 614, which is of similar size and purpose. The Yak-40 carries a flight crew of 2 and, in its initial production form, has standard seating for 24 or 27 passengers in a pressurised cabin. There is a let-down airstair door at the rear of the cabin, similar to that fitted to the Aérospatiale Caravelle.

The first of five development aircraft (CCCP-1966) flew on 21 October 1966, and production was started in the following year. By the end of 1967 twenty-four had been built. The Yak-40 flew its first scheduled passenger service for Aeroflot on 30 September 1968; within the next two and a half

years more than two hundred had been delivered, with production continuing at a rate of eight aircraft per month. By the beginning of 1970 the aircraft in service had carried a total of 230,000 passengers and collectively had flown some 5,592,300 miles (9,000,000 km). Aeroflot's short-haul local services cover several thousand routes, and in addition to passenger-carrying the Yak-40 is employed for ambulance and cargo transportation. An 8/10-seat executive version is also available. Weather radar and other equipment permit the aircraft to make automatic approaches in Category 2 weather conditions. Development of the Yak-40 undertaken to mid-1971 had included an increase in passenger capacity to 34 seats (or 40 if no baggage is carried), still within the same length fuselage, and the provision of a thrust reverser (protected by retractable clamshell doors) on the centre engine. Initial exports have been made, the first consisting of two aircraft for Aviaexport's Italian distributor, Aertirrena. Further sales were expected later in 1971.

64 Tupolev Tu-154 ('Careless')

In the past the western nations have had to assess the capabilities of any new Soviet aeroplane the hard way. Russian reticence has softened somewhat in recent years with regard to its civil aviation products, but never had a new design been announced with such a wealth of structural and performance data as the Tu-154. In its original form the Tu-154 was the largest tri-jet airliner planned for production anywhere in the world, and is intended to be developed to carry even greater loads. Primarily intended as a medium/long-range replacement for Aeroflot's An-10, Il-18 and Tu-104B fleet in the 1970s, the Tu-154 was first announced outside Russia in the spring of 1966, at which time a prototype and five pre-production aircraft were already under construction; the first of these (CCCP-85000) flew for the first time on 4 October 1968. The initial production model is a 128/158-seater, with a three- or four-man flight crew and a cabin staff of six. Operating estimates for this version claim that it will have only about half the direct operating costs of the Il-18 or Tu-104B, and that with less than half its seats filled will still be able to carry a big enough cargo load to achieve break-even load factors. Airfield performance is excellent, normal take-off distance being 3,740 ft (1,140 m) and landing runs being shortened by the use of thrust reversers on the two outer engines. Variants of the Tu-154 being developed include an all-freight version with a capacity payload of 44,090 lb (20,000 kg), and a stretched passenger model, the Tu-154M, which will seat up to 240 occupants. The obvious potential of the Tu-154 for expansion, coupled with the unprecedented publicity given to it by the Soviets, indicate that this 'Tupolev Trident' could become a serious contender in world markets within the near future. Entry into Aeroflot service was made on the Moscow-Tbilisi route in July 1971, at which time an initial export order was expected from CSA Czechoslovak Airlines for about six aircraft.

65 Lockheed L-1011 TriStar

Second of the new-generation widebody airbuses to be conceived in the United States, the Lockheed Model 193 TriStar had its origins in a 1966 study for a twin-turbofan 300-seat short/medium-range airliner for domestic routes, to meet a requirement of American Airlines; but by March 1968, when the development go-ahead was given, discussion with this and other American operators had resulted in Lockheed pursuing a tri-jet layout instead, using as powerplant the highly-promising Rolls-Royce RB. 211 turbofan engine. The development programme for the aircraft, named TriStar, originally involved six aircraft – later reduced to five – and construction of the first of these began in March 1969. Designated L-1011, and registered N1011, this aircraft flew for the first time on 16 November 1970; it was followed by N1012 on 15 February and N301EA on 17 May 1971. The fourth TriStar was due to fly later in 1971, and deliveries to begin in March 1972.

These aircraft are representative of the basic L-1011-1 short/medium-haul version (as illustrated), which carries a crew of 13, has seating for up to 345 passengers in an all-economy class layout, and will have an initial in-service gross weight of 430,000 lb (195,040 kg). Certification and first deliveries were due before the end of 1971. By mid-1971 orders and options had been received (though actual quantities had not been firmly fixed in all cases) from Delta, Eastern, PSA and TWA in the United States; and from the British-based Air Holdings company for resale to Air Canada, Air Jamaica and other non-US customers.

In September 1969 Lockheed also announced the L-1011-8, proposed as a long-range intercontinental version with later-model RB. 211 engines, a slightly lengthened fuselage (seating up to 400 passengers), enlarged wings and tail surfaces, and six-wheel main landing gear bogies. The go-ahead for this version was then declared conditional upon the receipt of orders, and its development – together with that of the whole TriStar programme – was further inhibited by the financial collapse of Rolls-Royce, with its consequent threat to the future of the RB. 211 engine, early in 1971. United States government support for the TriStar was obtained, by the hair's-breadth margin of a single vote, in August 1971. How this will affect the future of the L-1011-8 version remained to be seen, though it seemed possible that Lockheed might pursue the evolution of a somewhat less ambitious long-range model.

66 McDonnell Douglas DC-10

A design contemporary of the Lockheed TriStar, the McDonnell Douglas DC-10 established a small lead over its rival in terms of reaching the flight test stage – a lead which, with the powerplant supply difficulties that have affected development of the Lockheed aircraft, is likely to be substantially increased. The DC-10 responded, as did the TriStar, to an American Airlines requirement of early 1966 calling originally for a twin-turbofan short/medium-haul aircraft for domestic routes, but eventually matured into a three-engined design. McDonnell Douglas's choice of the General Electric CF6 turbofan has avoided the problems posed to Lockheed by the Rolls-Royce collapse, and construction of the first of five development aircraft was started in January 1969. This aircraft (N10DC) made its first flight on 10 August 1970 and was allocated to stability and control testing. The third aircraft (N102AA) was the next to fly, on 24 October 1970, and is the performance test machine. It was followed on 23 December 1970 by the second DC-10, and by mid-1971 all five aircraft were flying. FAA Type Approval was received, and the first two deliveries were made, on 29 July 1971; these were to American Airlines and United Air Lines, which both began services in mid-August, their aircraft having seating capacities of 206 and 222 respectively. Each airline was due to receive five aircraft by the end of 1971.

These are of the basic US domestic model, which is known as the Series 10 and has also been ordered by Continental Air Lines and National Airlines in the US. Sole customer for the Series 20, up to mid-1971, was Northwest Airlines. The Series 20 is a long-range intercontinental version, and is powered initially by 45,500 lb (20,640 kg) st Pratt &

Whitney JT9D-15 or 47,000 lb (21,318 kg) st JT9D-25 turbofan engines. The Series 30 is basically similar, but uses 48,100 lb (21,817 kg) st CF6-50A engines; customers include Air Afrique, Air New Zealand, Alitalia, the KUSS consortium, Lufthansa, Overseas National, Sabena, TIA and UTA. Those ordered by ONA, Sabena and TIA are cargo-convertible Series 30F; similar F models of the Series 10 and 20 are also available. Given its lead over the TriStar and the European A 300B, the DC-10 is well poised to acquire a substantial proportion of the airbus market, and could well become one of the most successful commercial transport aircraft of the 1970s.

67   Hawker Siddeley Comet 4

Even before the first of the Comet 1 accidents, de Havilland had made studies for a 'stretched' Comet 3, and work continued on this prototype notwithstanding the subsequent grounding and investigation of the earlier models. Registered G-ANLO, it flew for the first time on 19 July 1954, differing from earlier Comets in having a 111 ft 6 in (33·98 m) fuselage and 10,000 lb (4,536 kg) st Avon 502 engines. Additional fuel was carried in leading-edge pinion tanks, and the gross weight was increased by some 25,000 lb (11,340 kg) over the Comet 2. By the end of 1954, however, with the full accident findings available, de Havilland decided to combine all the latest knowledge into a Mk 4 version; and a modified G-ANLO, now with Avon 523's,

began the flight test programme for this model in February 1957. The two Comet 2E's, G-AMXD and 'XK, had meanwhile continued the Avon development flying programme with a 7,330 lb (3,325 kg) st Avon 504 in each inner position, and a 10,500 lb (4,763 kg) st Avon 524 in each outer one; and these two aircraft assisted further by flying an extensive route-proving programme during 1957–58. The first production Comet 4 (G-APDA), flown on 27 April 1958, was the first of nineteen ordered by BOAC: Aerolineas Argentinas ordered six others, and East African Airways three. Although originally meant for Commonwealth and Far Eastern services, New York was within the range of the Comet 4, and BOAC became involved in a race to beat Pan American (with the Boeing 707) in being the first with fare-paying jet services across the North Atlantic. The British airline, which opened its London–New York route on 4 October 1958, was the winner by some three weeks. Later, the Comet 4's were widely used in their intended territories, both by BOAC and by such associates as Air-India, Nigerian Airways and Qantas. By comparison with the Comet 1/1A's, the Comet 4's, during their first two years of operation, flew some sixty-eight thousand revenue hours. The projected 70/92-seat Comet 4A for Capital Airlines, with 3 ft 4 in (1·01 m) longer fuselage and the wing cropped by 7 ft 0 in (2·13 m), was not built, but the same wing, minus the pinion tanks and mounting 10,500 lb (4,763 kg) st Avon 525B engines, was used for the Comet 4B ordered by BEA for short- and medium-haul routes. A further stretch of the fuselage to 118 ft 0 in (35·97 m) enabled the Comet 4B to seat up to 101 passengers. Fourteen 4B's were ultimately ordered by BEA, the first of these (G-APMA) flying on 27 June 1959; four others, with an 86-seat layout, entered service with Olympic Airways in 1960. Marriage of the 4B fuselage and seating capacity with the original full-span wing of the Comet 4 produced the final Comet version, the 4C, which flew for the first time (G-AOVU) on 31 October 1959. This version was purchased by Aerolineas Argentinas (one), Kuwait Airways (two), Mexicana (three), Middle East Airlines (four), Sudan Airways (two) and United Arab Airlines (nine). When Comet production came to an end, a total of seventy-four Series 4's had been built, including military and VIP transports; forty-three were still in airline service in 1970.

68 & 73 **Boeing 707/720 series**
Boeing began to think seriously about a future jet airliner immediately after the end of World War 2, and made tentative approaches to selected potential customers in 1950. Before another two years had elapsed the company had decided in principle to start work on a private venture design capable of developing into both a passenger successor to the Stratocruiser and a jet tanker successor to its military counterpart, the KC-97. Developed initially under the designation Model 367-

80, the prototype (9,500 lb (4,309 kg) st JT3P engines) was rolled out on 14 May 1954 and made its first flight on 15 July, its true identity being revealed by its civil registration N70700. Only three months later the USAF ordered a substantial number of KC-135 tankers, and the first order for the airliner version came on 13 October 1955 when Pan American ordered six 707-121's. (The 707 family are identified by basic 'dash' numbers, those in the -120 and -220 blocks being domestic models and those in the -320 and -420 blocks being intercontinental versions. Customer configurations in each series begin at '21; a B suffix indicates turbofan engines instead of turbojets, and a C suffix denotes a B model with cargo-carrying capability.)

The production 707-120, the basic domestic version, is somewhat larger than the original prototype. Qantas 707-138's are unique in this series in having a 134 ft 6 in (41·00 m) overall length; all other 707-120's are 144 ft 6 in (44·04 m) overall. The first production -120 flew on 20 December 1957 and was delivered to Pan American in the following August. On 26 October 1958 PanAm put its Boeings into operaton on the New York–London route. The 707-120 was powered by 13,500 lb (6,124 kg) st JT3C-6 turbojet engines, but all those in service (except those of Continental Airlines and TWA) are of 707-120B standard with 17,000 lb (7,711 kg) st JT3D-1 or 18,000 lb (8,165 kg) st JT3D-3 turbofans. The first aircraft converted in this way, for

American Airlines, was flown for the first time with turbofans on 22 June 1960. Three VC-137A transports with Military Airlift Command were similarly converted to fan-engined VC-137B's. Domestic 707 variants – other than the 720, which is described later – were completed by the 707-220, a reduced-weight version of the -120 powered by 15,800 lb (7,167 kg) st JT4A-3 turbojets and having a better 'hot and high' airfield performance. Five 707-220's were built, all for Braniff, bringing total production of the above-mentioned versions to one hundred and forty-one. Seventeen years after its first appearance, the original 'Dash Eighty' prototype is still flying as a testbed for various members of the Boeing jet airliner family.

Although the original -120's of Pan American opened the airline career of the Boeing 707 by flying on the North Atlantic route, the decision to use it across the Atlantic was taken more for prestige than for practical operating reasons; and, having made its point, the 707-120 reverted to the US internal network for which it was tailored. The genuine international model is the 707-320 Intercontinental, which flew for the first time on 11 January 1959. This is a much larger aeroplane, with wing span increased by 11 ft 7 in (3·43 m) and overall length by 8 ft 5 in (2·56 m) compared with the domestic -120 model, and more powerful JT4A turbojet engines. Pan American was also the first to buy the Intercontinental version, beginning ser-

vices across the United States on 26 August 1959 and across the North Atlantic on 10 October. Another early customer for the long-range model was BOAC, which created a new 707 series, the -420, by specifying 17,500 lb (7,938 kg) st Rolls-Royce Conway 508 turbofans for its Boeings. The first Conway-powered 707 flew on 20 May 1959, and after evaluating the first four aircraft, BOAC requested modifications to enhance the stability and control, including an increase of 2 ft 11 in (0·89 m) in fin height, combined with additional fin area beneath the fuselage tail cone. These features were subsequently incorporated in most of the -320's and many of the earlier series aircraft built. The first -420 services by BOAC commenced in May 1960, and four other airlines also operated this version. Sixty-nine 707-320's and thirty-seven -420's were built. Inevitably, with the additional performance and carrying capacity made possible by the use of turbofan powerplants, a fan-engined variant of the -320 was not long in making its appearance in the United States. This was the -320B, first flown on 31 January 1962 and employing the JT3D-3 engine of 18,000 lb (8,165 kg) thrust. An additional feature of the -320B was the introduction of new minimum-drag wingtips, which increased the overall span by a further 3 ft 4 in (1·01 m). The 707-320B remains in production, as does the 707-320C, which appeared a year later; the latter is a passenger and/or cargo version of the B, distinguished by a large freight-loading door ahead of the wing on the port side. The -320C has proved the most popular of all the Intercontinental versions, whose combined order book up to 30 April 1971 totalled five hundred and sixty-one.

The trio of basic Boeing 707 models was completed in July 1957, when Boeing announced an intermediate-range version. The new arrival was, in terms of structure and weight, virtually a fresh design; and this fact was acknowledged in November 1957, when, concurrently with the news of its first order (from United Air Lines for eleven aircraft), the designation Boeing 720 was allocated. Dimensionally, the 720 is close to the 707-120, having a fuselage shorter by 7 ft 9 in (2·36 m) and an identical wing span. The wings, however, have slightly more sweep inboard than the other Boeings and full-span leading-edge flaps which enhance the 720's airfield performance. Powerplant is four JT3C series turbojets. The first Boeing 720 was flown on 23 November 1959, received operating approval from the FAA in June 1960 and entered service with United on 5 July 1960. A total of fifty-five were built for six customers, United being the major operator with an eventual fleet of twenty-nine. A fan-engined counterpart, the Boeing 720B, appeared in 1960. With JT3D series engines, the first aircraft of this type was flown on 6 October 1960 and received FAA type approval in March 1961. The first customer for the 720B was American Airlines, who put it into service on 12 March 1961. Combined production of the 720 and 720B, which ended in 1969, totalled one hundred and fifty-four.

69 McDonnell Douglas DC-8

The DC-8, which began life as the Douglas Model 1881, was announced in June 1955 and became available to the airlines about a year later than the first Boeing 707's. The decision to proceed with what was then envisaged as a domestic airliner was followed in October 1955 by the first order (from Pan American) for twenty-five. By the end of 1955 an intercontinental model had also been proposed, and Douglas had received DC-8 orders from three more US airlines, two in Europe and one in Japan. By 30 May 1958, when the JT3C-powered prototype (N8008D) made its first flight, the order book stood at more than a hundred and thirty aircraft. Standard DC-8's were built in five basic versions, two for domestic routes and three for intercontinental operation. The domestic models are the Series 10 with 13,500 lb (6,124 kg) st JT3C-6 turbojets, and the Series 20 powered by 15,800 lb (7,167 kg) st JT4A-3's. The intercontinental Series 30 offers a choice of JT4A-9 or -11 engines; the Series 40, Rolls-Royce Conway 509's of 17,500 lb (7,945 kg) st; and the Series 50 has JT3D-1 or -3 turbofans. Laterproduction Series 50's, designated Model 55, have detail airframe improvements and JT3D-3B turbofans. The first DC-8-20 was flown on 29 November 1958, the DC-8-30 and -40 on 21 February and 23 July 1959, and the first DC-8-50 on 20 December 1960. The DC-8-10 was the first model to go into operation, entering service simultaneously with United and Delta on 18 September 1959. Meanwhile, Douglas had introduced drag-reducing modifications to the wing which involved a new leading-edge and wingtip profile with leading edge slots. A DC-8-40 thus modified made, on 21 August 1961, the first flight at over Mach 1 by a jet airliner when it reached 667 mph (1,073 km/hr) in a shallow dive, equivalent to Mach 1·012. Numerically, the most successful variant has been the Series 50, and some domestic-model DC-8's have since been converted to this standard. In April 1961, Douglas announced a further variant, the DC-8F Jet Trader, which is an all-cargo or mixed-traffic version of the Series 50 with JT3D-3 fan engines, reinforced floor and increased gross weight. The first DC-8F was flown on 29 October 1962, and this version is available in basic form as the DC-8-54 and, in improved form, with JT3D-3B engines, as the DC-8-55. Maximum capacity of the Jet Trader is 95,282 lb (43,219 kg) or 189 passengers. Excluding the 'Super Sixty' variants, described separately, two hundred and ninety-four DC-8's (twenty-eight -10's, thirty-four -20's, fifty-seven -30's, thirty-two -40's, eighty-nine -50's and fifty-four -54/55's) were built before production ended in November 1968.

70 **Convair 880**

Although seating fewer passengers than the Boeing 707 or Douglas DC-8, the Convair 880 on its first appearance offered a better speed performance than its rivals. Its existence was announced in the spring of 1956, at which time it was known as the Convair 600 Skylark, with the news that TWA and Delta had ordered thirty and ten respectively. Soon afterwards the name was changed to Golden Arrow, reflecting a colourful if somewhat bizarre proposal to use gold-tinted skin panels in the aeroplane's construction. This proposal was short-lived, however, and the aeroplane was again re-designated, this time as the Convair 880 Model 22, the title Convair 600 being retained temporarily for a stretched version. The Model 22 became the standard US domestic version, and flew for the first time on 27 January 1959 with four 11,200 lb (5,081 kg) st CJ805-3 turbojet engines. First delivery of a production 880 was made on 31 January 1960 to Delta Air Lines, which introduced the aeroplane into service on 15 May, exactly two weeks after the granting of its FAA type certificate. A few of the TWA aircraft were leased to Northeast Airlines, which started services a month earlier than TWA, in December 1960. Two months before this, on 3 October 1960, the first flight had taken place of the original 880 prototype modified for service on intercontinental routes. This version, originating as the Convair 880 Model 31, carried substantially more fuel but offered the same accommodation as the domestic version. With a certain amount of its extra range sacrificed in favour of improvements designed to give better airfield performance and quicker turn-round times, the Model 31 was redesignated 880-M in October 1959. New features included leading-edge wing slats, increased fin area and CJ805-3B turbojets. Gross weight was increased from 184,500 lb (83,691 kg) in the domestic 880 to 203,400 lb (92,262 kg) in the 880-M, and maximum payload from 27,600 lb (12,519 kg) to 33,600 lb (15,241 kg). Standard seating in both models ranges from 88 to 110 passengers, with a maximum possible of 124. The first delivery of a Convair 880-M was made to CAT, the Chinese Nationalist airline, in June 1961, airline operations beginning shortly after the issue of an FAA type certificate on 24 July. Convair 880-M's were ordered in small numbers by a few foreign operators, but neither this version nor its domestic counterpart competed very successfully against the Boeing or Douglas jets and only sixty-five examples of the two models were completed.

71 Tupolev Tu-144 ('Charger')

It was obvious, even without positive confirmation, that the Soviet Union would not be left out of the race to develop and put into service a supersonic passenger aircraft. The confirmation came at the 1965 Salon de l'Aéronautique in Paris, where the Russians displayed a model of their proposed design, the Tu-144; and subsequently Andrei Tupolev himself publicly expressed his desire to have a prototype in the air ahead of the Anglo-French Concorde.

There is much superficial similarity of outline between the Concorde and the Tu-144, each employing an ogival (dual-curve) delta wing and a 'droop-snoot' nose section which hinges down for landing and incorporates a retractable flight deck visor. The Tu-144 wings – on the prototype at least – are however less complex aerodynamically; the vertical tail area is proportionally greater, and the fuselage underside is flatter, than on the Concorde. A major external difference lies in the power installation, that of the Tu-144 comprising four afterburning Kuznetsov turbofans (the Concorde has turbojets) grouped together in pairs beneath the fuselage, each pair having a bifurcated, area-ruled exhaust duct and variable-geometry intakes. All four engines have reheat, to boost the take-off climb, and the outer two are fitted with thrust reversers. Design of the Tu-144 was led by Andrei Tupolev's son, Professor Alexei Andreievich Tupolev, and the USSR has, like the manufacturers of the Concorde, flight-tested a scaled-down wing on a special research aircraft. A reduction in the capacity of the Tu-144 was noted in 1966: the original model shown at Le Bourget in the previous year had revealed a 36-seat forward cabin, galley amidships and a 90-seat rear cabin. In June 1966 Andrei Tupolev referred to the aircraft as a 121-seater, and the latest details available by mid-1971 showed alternative arrangements for 18 or 40 persons in the forward cabin, with seats for 80 in the rear cabin in each case.

In service, the aircraft will carry a flight crew of three.

Tupolev's ambition to beat the Concorde into the air was realised on 31 December 1968, when the first Tu-144 prototype (CCCP-68001) became the first supersonic transport aircraft to fly. This occasion was also, incidentally, the first time that the NK-144 engines had been tested in the air. On 21 May 1970 the aircraft made its public début at Moscow's Sheremetievo Airport, and five days later it became the world's first SST to fly at a speed in excess of Mach 2, actually achieving a speed of 1,336 mph (2,150 km/hr). By the time another twelve months had elapsed – when it made its first appearance to a western public at the 1971 Paris Salon – the Tu-144 had reached speeds of up to 1,518 mph (2,443 km/hr) during trials. At this time it was declared that only one aircraft had flown, but in October 1971 reports indicated that two more Tu-144s had been completed and begun flight testing. These are presumably pre-production aircraft, and may incorporate several modifications such as higher-powered engines with more efficient intakes, modified wing leading edges and refined wing-tips. The first production aircraft should be completed by the end of 1972, with entry into Aeroflot service following in 1973–74. The Soviet airline has said that the Tu-144 will be flown at subsonic speeds for some 40 per cent of the time on its domestic network; it will also be operated on international services and will be available for export. It is considered by western observers that the Soviet design, although in many ways less refined than that of the Concorde, has a greater 'stretch' potential than the Anglo-French type.

72 Aérospatiale/BAC Concorde

As an example of international collaboration the Concorde provides evidence in the most convincing form that associations of this kind can compete on at least equal terms with the giant aircraft-producing systems of Russia and the United States. Development and production of the west's first supersonic airliner is a fifty-fifty joint undertaking by England and France, for which formal agreements were signed at the end of November 1962. It incorporates background research conducted by the RAE in Britain in the mid-1950s into the properties of slim-delta wings, and inherits some of the design features of the 'Super Caravelle' displayed in model form by Sud-Aviation at the 1961 Paris Air Show. Intended for flight at Mach 2·2, the Concorde employs an ogival (dual-curve) wing plan-form whose characteristics have been tested extensively on the BAC-221, rebuilt from the record-breaking Fairey Delta 2 of 1956. Low-speed handling characteristics have similarly been determined from evaluation of the Handley Page H.P. 115 slim-delta research aircraft. Power is provided by a Rolls-Royce/ SNECMA development of the Bristol Siddeley Olympus turbojet which powered the Vulcan bomber. This engine is being developed to give an initial in-service thrust (Mk 602) of 38,050 lb (17,260 kg) with 17 per cent reheat, rising to 39,940 lb (18,116 kg) in the Mk 612 engine which will become available some two years later. All four engines will be fitted with thrust reversers. Six aircraft, including two for structural testing, are involved in the development programme. Aérospatiale has responsibility for the first (prototype), third (static test) and fifth (pre-production) machines, and BAC for the second (prototype), fourth (pre-production) and sixth (static test) aircraft. The prototypes both have 'contrived' registrations, the French-built 001 being F-WTSS (Transport SuperSonique) and the British-built 002 G-BSST (British SuperSonic Transport). First flights were made on 2 March 1969 (001 at Toulouse) and 9 April 1969 (002 at Bristol) respectively. In 1964 the development potential of the Olympus 593 series engines permitted a slight scaling-up of the overall design, making possible an increase of 19 ft 3½ in (5·90 m) in passenger cabin length and standard seating for 128 people (maximum 144). The Concorde is, however, being offered with a basic 112-seat single-class layout, with which profitable operation is foreseen at fares some 15 per cent below the standard first-class rates. The two pre-series aircraft reflect this increase, and the 02 will be virtually representative of the production version, with elongated tail-cone and other modifications. The Concorde 01 (G-AXDN) had been completed by the spring of 1971, and its maiden

flight was expected in October; the 02 was due to fly in France in 1973, followed by the first production aircraft, also in France, in January 1973. Deliveries to airlines (sixteen of whom had options on a total of seventy-four Concordes) are due to begin in the spring of 1974. Air France, BOAC and Pan American are expected to be the first Concorde operators. By mid-1971 Anglo-French government approval had been extended to give the go-ahead for manufacture of the first ten production aircraft (plus the ordering of materials and equipment for the next six), and all sixteen airlines had renewed their options to await the completion of the development programme.

This programme had proceeded in a completely satisfactory manner with the two prototype aircraft, Mach 1 first being exceeded on 1 October 1969 and Mach 2 on 4 November 1970, by Concorde 001 on each occasion. Both prototypes have since been flown at well over Mach 2, and by mid-July 1971 these two aircraft had made 288 flights, representing a total of 593 hours, including 155½ hours at supersonic speeds.

74 Convair 990A

The first proposals for an elongated and faster version of the Convair 600 (as it then was) were put forward in the early months of 1958. The desired increase in performance was to be obtained by aerodynamic improvements and the employment of a turbofan powerplant; while the increase in passenger capacity would be achieved by a 10 ft 0 in (3·05 m) overall lengthening of the fuselage. Convair remained faithful to General Electric in its choice of engine, selecting the CJ805-23B to power the new model; and, apart from the stretching of the fuselage, most of the aerodynamic changes involved the engine and mainplane layout. A thinner aerofoil section was achieved by retaining the same actual thickness while increasing the wing's chord and thereby its gross area. Area-ruled anti-shock fairings were added to the trailing edge primarily to enhance the aeroplane's high-speed cruising capabilities, though they provided additional fuel storage as well; and full-span leading-edge flaps were fitted. Originally known as the Convair 600 Model 30, development was somewhat protracted, and the designation was amended to Convair 990 to avoid the implication that it was an earlier design than the 880. There was no separate 990 prototype, the first flight being made, on 24 January 1961, by the first of twenty aircraft ordered by American Airlines. The first delivery to the airline, some three weeks after the 990 was certificated by the FAA, was made on 7 January 1962. Swissair, which named the aircraft Coronado, received its first delivery at about the same time and was actually the first airline to begin operating the type, towards the end of February; American began its 990 services, between New York and Chicago, on 18 March. Flight testing of the 990 during 1961 had revealed a number of aerodynamic

shortcomings, one solution to which was to shorten the outboard engine pylons to reduce drag; other refinements deemed necessary after subsequent testing and operating experience included further streamlining of the pylons and the installation of full-span Krueger flaps on the underside of the wing leading edge. With these modifications, duly carried out on all thirty-seven 990's built, the aircraft became known as the Convair 990A. Fresh FAA certificates for the 990A were granted in October 1962 for those serving abroad and in January 1963 for the domestically operated aircraft.

75 BAC VC10 and Super VC10

Probably no airliner since the Viscount has evoked such enthusiasm from its passengers as the VC10 when it entered BOAC service in 1964. Few, since the Comet and the Caravelle, have had the VC10's aesthetic appeal; and when airline pilots – rarely given to effusive praise of the machines they have to fly – utter such phrases as 'thoroughly delightful to handle in every respect' it is safe to assume that the aeroplane in question is a cut above the average. Yet, despite this widespread appeal, the VC10's sales record was disappointing, for only fifty-five were sold, and only nine to foreign customers. To some extent this was because the VC10 was tailored closely – some would say too closely – to the requirements of BOAC and the Royal Air Force. It was in the mid-1950s that BOAC first outlined its requirements for a

Comet successor on its African and Far Eastern routes. Vickers had already studied a number of jet airliner possibilities, including the Type 100 and the so-called 'Vanjet', a Conway-powered development of the Vanguard with swept wings. In May 1957, after further discussions between manufacturer and customer, BOAC confirmed its intention to order the VC10. Detailed design began in the spring of 1958, and construction of a Model 1100 prototype (G-ARTA) in January 1959. This made its maiden flight on 29 June 1962, powered by four 21,000 lb (9,525 kg) st Conway RCo. 42 turbofan engines. Twelve similarly-powered Model 1101's were completed for BOAC, and began operations, on the service to Lagos, on 29 April 1964, six days after the award of an ARB certificate. Other VC10's include the Model 1102 (two for Ghana Airways) and the 1103 (three for British United); these were fitted with a large cargo door in the port side of the forward fuselage, and have increased chord at the wing roots. Save for their engines (RCo. 43's) and added fuel tankage, the fourteen 1106's for Air Support Command are generally similar, though interior equipment and operating weights naturally differ. The original BOAC order had been for thirty-five VC10's, which was later cut to twelve to enable the airline to order thirty of a stretched version, the Super VC10, but under government pressure this order for Supers was later limited to seventeen aircraft. Compared with the stand-ard VC10, the Super is 13 ft 0 in (3·96 m) longer; seats a maximum of 174 passengers; has RCo. 43 engines, with thrust reversers on all four (instead of just the outer two). The first Super VC10 (G-ASGA) was flown on 7 May 1964. The Super VC10's of BOAC have the Model number 1151 and are all-passenger aircraft. East African Airways' 1154's have a mixed cargo/passenger layout and forward freight door. Standard VC10's have been in service with Caledonian/BUA since November 1964, serving South America, Africa and the Middle East, and with Ghana Airways since February 1965. The first BOAC service with Super VC10's commenced on 1 April 1965.

76 Ilyushin Il-62 ('Classic')

In the post-Stalin atmosphere of economic, as well as military, competition between Soviet Russia and the western nations, there have been several examples of the 'date' of an airliner being worked into the designation or prototype registration. One may guess, therefore, that the leap from 18 to 62 in the design bureau numbers of Sergei Ilyushin's two most recent commercial airliners is explained by the fact that the prototype of this elegant newcomer (CCCP-06156) emerged for the first time in 1962 – actually on 24 September, when it was inspected by Premier Krushchev. The neat lines and general configuration of this long-haul Soviet airliner obviously invite comparison with the British Super VC10, and the power of its NK-8 turbofans compares closely with the Conways of the British aeroplane. Early flight trials of the Il-62, pending availability of the definitive NK-8 engines, were conducted with two prototype and three pre-series aircraft powered initially by 16,535 lb (7,500 kg) st Lyulka AL-7 turbojets; the maiden flight, in the hands of veteran test pilot Vladimir Kokkinaki, took place in January 1963. Public début came at Vnukovo in the spring of 1965, and the aircraft displayed at Le Bourget in June (CCCP-06176, believed to be the third machine) had by then been re-engined with Kuznetsov turbofans. Other minor changes noted at this time included an extension of the drooped wing leading edge and a shorter nosewheel leg. Production of the Il-62 was initiated in 1965, the type entering Aeroflot international service on the Moscow–Montreal route on 15 September 1967. Four alternative interior layouts are available, ranging from an 85-passenger international sleeper version to an all-economy class with 186 seats. Seating is from four to six abreast according to variant. The Aeroflot fleet was estimated to number about fifty of these aircraft at the end of 1970; foreign operators include CSA and Interflug, each with three.

In 1970 there appeared a higher-capacity, longer-range version known as the Il-62M-200. This seats up to 198 passengers in a fuselage unchanged dimensionally from the standard Il-62, and has an additional fuel tank installed in the fin. Major outward changes are the deletion of the wingtip fairings,

reducing the overall span to 139 ft 5¼ in (42·50 m), and the installation of 25,350 lb (11,500 kg) st Soloviev D-30-KU turbofan engines, increasing the range with a maximum 50,700 lb (23,000 kg) payload to 4,970 miles (8,000 km).

77 Boeing 747

The Boeing 747 is the outcome of several years' effort to produce a counter to the Super Sixty series of stretched Douglas DC-8's. Until 1965 Boeing was still canvassing potential customers in an endeavour to meet this threat by variously enlarged versions of the 720-320B, but by the beginning of 1966 it was evident that this idea had been abandoned in favour of what has since become popularly known as the 'jumbo jet', the Boeing 747. Although in terms of general configuration the 747 clearly followed the highly successful layout of the 707 series, it is nearly 80 ft (24·38 m) longer and has treble the capacity of the 707-320B. Into the 747 went much of the design thought and work originally given to Boeing's unsuccessful contender for the giant C-5A military contract. From the beginning the Boeing 747 was designed to be equally viable whether carrying passengers or cargo, and Boeing expect about half the ultimate 747 sales to be of freighter versions. Originally proposed with a two-deck 'double-bubble' fuselage, the 747 design eventually became a single-decker, seating 374 people in the basic passenger model with a maximum possible load of 490 passengers. The first order was received from Pan American, which in April 1966 booked twenty-three all-passenger 747's and two 747F freighters. For the first half of the year this was Boeing's only order for the jumbo transport, but interest subsequently quickened and by the end of the year over eighty had been demanded. These included the first contract – from Continental Airlines – for the third variant, the convertible passenger/cargo 747C. There was no 747 prototype as such, the first flight being made by a production aircraft on 9 February 1969. Type approval was granted by the FAA on 30 December 1969, and the 'jumbo' entered passenger service on 22 January 1970 on Pan American's route between New York and London. With eight-abreast seating in a 20 ft 0 in (6·10 m) wide, 185 ft 0 in (56·39 m) long cabin with 8 ft 4 in (2·54 m) headroom, the Boeing 747 has, quite literally, brought a new dimension to air travel – though the very spaciousness, coupled with the much greater number of passengers requiring attention, has created some new internal logistics problems for the cabin staffs. Total 747 orders, up to 30 April 1971, were for two hundred and four, of which some 60 per cent had been delivered. The initial model is designated 747-100; the later 747-200 (first flight 11 October 1970) has increased operating weights, more powerful JT9D-7 engines, and is available in B (passenger), C (convertible) and F (cargo) configurations. The C and F models have an upward-hinged nose cone to allow straight-in loading of bulky freight items. The first 747-200 operator was KLM, which introduced this version into service in 1971.

78 McDonnell Douglas DC-8 Super Sixty series

Three stretched and improved variants of the DC-8 have made a substantial contribution to the total order book for this four-jet transport since the first details were announced in April 1965. Under the generic title 'Super Sixty', these comprise the DC-8-61, -62 and -63, all of which have the same powerplant and exist in passenger, cargo or mixed-traffic layouts. First in service (with United Air Lines, from November 1966) was the DC-8-61, which has a fuselage 36 ft 8 in (11·17 m) longer than the standard DC-8-50, seating up to 259 passengers and providing additional baggage/cargo space. Primarily a high-density domestic model, the DC-8-61 was flown for the first time on 14 March 1966 and received its type certification from the FAA on 2 September. The maiden flight of the DC-8-62 took place on 29 August 1966, and this is a much more drastically redesigned version. Although its 189-passenger fuselage is only 6 ft 8 in (2·03 m) longer than the DC-8-50, it has longer, re-positioned engine pods and new drag-reducing wingtip extensions which increase the overall span by 6 ft 0 in (1·83 m). The internal wing structure has also been modified to increase fuel tankage for ultra-long ranges. Certification of the DC-8-62 was granted in April 1967, with first deliveries (to SAS) taking place on 3 May 1967 and entry into service on 22 May. By then the first flight had taken place (on 10 April 1967) of the DC-8-63, which combines the long fuselage of the -61 with the new wings and other aerodynamic refinements of the -62 and is the heaviest of all the many DC-8 variants, with a maximum take-off weight of 350,000 lb (158,760 kg). Certification of the DC-8-63 was granted on 30 June 1967; the first deliveries were PH-DEA *Amerigo Vespucci* and -DEB *Christopher Columbus* for KLM, with whom the Super 63 entered service on 27 July 1967. The DC-8-63 prototype flew with JT3D-3B turbo-fan engines, but most of those ordered subsequently have been fitted with JT3D-7's of 19,000 lb (8,618 kg) st each. 'Jet Trader' (all-freight or passenger/freight) versions are available of each Super Sixty model, and are identified by CF or F designation suffix letters. Largest single operator of Super Sixties is United, with orders for thirty 61's and ten 62's; other operators to have ordered ten or more include Air Canada, Alitalia, Delta, Eastern, Flying Tiger, KLM, SAS and Seaboard World. Total Super Sixty orders had exceeded two hundred and seventy-five by the end of 1970, at which time the -62 and -63 were the only DC-8 models still in production.

INDEX

The reference numbers refer to the illustrations and corresponding text.